MOTOR CYCLE RACING

MOTOR CYCLE RACING

BY PETER CARRICK

PAUL HAMLYN
LONDON/NEW YORK
SYDNEY/TORONTO

Devised and designed by Haydon Young

Published 1969 by
The Hamlyn Publishing Group Ltd
London / New York / Sydney / Toronto
Hamlyn House, The Centre, Feltham, Middlesex
© 1969 by The Hamlyn Publishing Group Ltd
Printed in Italy by Arnoldo Mondadori Editore, Verona

CONTENTS

LEAP INTO THE SADDLE

The inevitability of motor cycle sport was established when two major inventions, the wheel and the internal combustion engine, came together. That was in 1875 when Siegfried Markus, an Austrian, produced his power-driven four-wheeler.

In 1885 Karl Benz of Mannheim developed a three-wheel vehicle driven by a single-cylinder internal combustion engine and in that same year, Gottlieb Daimler, another German, introduced his historic two-wheel boneshaker.

The world's first motor cycle had arrived.

It would be almost unrecognizable among today's high-powered, sophisticated machines. The engine was a single-cylinder, air-cooled, four-stroke developed by Daimler. He had earlier worked with Germany's Dr Otto, who in 1876 had patented the four-stroke principle. It was mounted vertically between two enormous wheels. Remarkably, perhaps, the unveiling of Daimler's trendsetter was still some twenty years before the first motor cycle race of any significance was held, near Paris, in 1904.

Even in Daimler's time names which were to become part of the history of motor cycle sport had already moved into focus. John Boyd Dunlop had developed his pneumatic tyre as early as 1888 and in 1903 a Dunlop advertisement proclaimed: '18,000 miles on a

1

1 Pioneer racer Harry Martin astride his record-breaking
2¾ h.p. Excelsior machine of 1903. At Canning Town cycle track
he did a mile, from a standing start, in 1 min. 24 secs.

2 Dr. Nikolaus Otto;
3 Gottlieb Daimler, inventor of the first motor cycle;
4 Karl Benz, who died in 1929;
5 Siegfried Markus, producer of a power-driven four wheeler
in 1875.

motor cycle fitted with one pair of Dunlop tyres'. Hans Renolds introduced the roller chain in 1894, and in 1898 a certain James L. Norton began business as a chain manufacturer. Thirty-five years later the brilliant racing machines bearing his name were sweeping to world-wide supremacy, dictating a chapter of motor cycle history unparalleled even today.

The development of the motor cycle in its present form started at the turn of the century. Motor cycling, even of the extremely domestic kind, was an unpredictable adventure. With little engine power and no variable gearing, the rider had to depend on his pedalling gear to break the crests of hills, and skidding was an inevitable danger because of the eccentricities of the steering of these high-built machines with their puny tyres. But the most intrepid of these stalwart pioneer riders pulled their cloth caps firmly on their heads, squatted low and made it a roaring, reckless sport too. Pedal cycle clubs began to form motor cycle sections with special-attraction events on club programmes.

As early as 1897 the Horseless Vehicle Journal, reporting a race between a motor cycle and an ordinary pedal cycle, disclosed: 'W. J. Stocks on the cycle covered 27 miles 300 yards in an hour. Although the motor bicycle ran splendidly throughout, soon after the start the motor slowed down and the crowd jeered immensely, for they imagined its end had come. The cause of the pulling up, however, was that the rider thought from the shouting of the crowd that some mishap had oc-red, and he requested that they be kept quiet. Although at the finish the motor was 300 yards behind, he would be a bold man who declared that the cycle will always be able to beat the motor'. A shrewd observation indeed!

Europe was the mecca of motor cycle sport: the work of the early German and French inventors such as Count Albert de Dion, M. Georges Bouton, the Hildebrand brothers and Alois Wolfmuller, saw to that. A more spirited development of motor cycling as a sport was severely hindered in Great Britain by road speed

limits of 4 m.p.h., then 12 m.p.h. and later 20 m.p.h. These were crippling, for even by this time machines had been developed which were capable of top speeds approaching 60 m.p.h. Early and now legendary characters like the Collier brothers were forced to race on cycle tracks to gain experience and to test their machines; and cycle tracks were far from adequate testing grounds for motorized sport, even in the early 1900s.

On both sides of the Channel, however, the competitive spirit was strong and riders began to battle for national honour. One of these early races was between Barden of England and Fournier of France, at the Canning Town cycle track. There were to be five races. The stake was £1,000. Only three of the races took place because Fournier decisively won all three and so won the series without having to compete further. Enthusiastic spectators, it is worth noting, were dressed in the track-side style of the day, bowlers and suits: caps and Norfolk jackets struck a more informal note which was later to predominate. The Canning Town cycle track was the background to many of these early speed events in Britain. There were 5-mile handicap races there in 1903 and in that same year, world-record breaker Harry Martin rode a 2¾ h.p. Excelsior at full blast to do a mile, from a standing start, in 1 min. 24 secs., an outstanding performance.

The Continental enthusiasts applied all their energy and ingenuity to the building of special 'race' machines constructed for outright speed, while elsewhere reliability was regarded as being more important. There developed a clash of ideals and ideas and the Continental machines were branded as monstrosities, by Britain in particular. Harry Martin's machine, for instance, was proudly proclaimed as 'a motor bicycle, not a monstrosity, as are so many record beaking instruments'.

Maurice Fournier's 22 h.p. machine of 1903, on the other hand, certainly qualified as one of these 'speed monstrosities' and reports that it was capable of attaining a speed of 80 m.p.h. shattered and shocked motorsport enthusiasts in England. It had a 2,340 c.c. twin-

6 Barden of England and Fournier of France battle for supremacy in one of the speed events held at the Canning Town track in 1903. Fournier won all three races.

7 The three-wheelers wait as MM. de Dion and Osmont prepare for the start of the 100 kilometres race in the *criterium des motocycles* in France in 1899. Great excitement prevailed at such events.

8 Harry Martin and F. Daynell on the first Martin machines.

9

10

11

12

9 Edward Butler's petrol-driven motor cycle of 1887.

10 The 1,830 c.c. Hildebrand & Wolfmuller machine of 1894.

11 Daimler's historic motor cycle of 1885—the boneshaker.

12 M. Echard (left), before the start of the Paris-Madrid race of 1903.

13 A White-Paffe engine powered this typical example of the machines competing in handicap events at the Canning Town track.

14 The Ormonde machine ridden by A. E. Wright in the ill-fated Paris-Madrid race. The built-up pulley, small saddle and other aids to lightness were the result of a 50 kg weight limit.

15 This French lady's motor cycle of 1903, used for hill-climbs, features a long inlet pipe to the wick carburettor in the tank; an advance and retard lever on the top tube is the only speed control.

16 Fossier and his massive pacing machine at the Parc des Princes track at Paris in 1903.

17 The Werner motor cycle ridden by M. Arnott in the Paris-Madrid race.

18 M. Lamberjack, of the highly successful Griffon team of 1903; this lightweight model was good for 60 m.p.h.

19 Marius The, 1904 World (Track) Champion, with his huge Buchet-engined vertical-twin machine.

20 Lawson, a French rider of 1904, with his cycle pacing machine. He is wearing the new-style inflatable crash-hat.

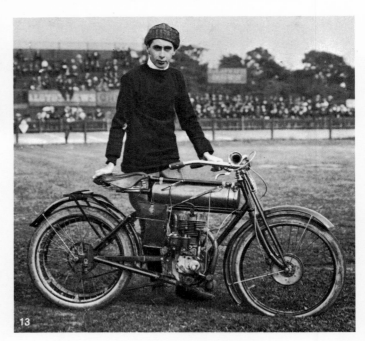

13

14

15

18

16

19

17

20

21 Rem Fowler, winner of the twin-cylinder class in the first TT race, in 1907, stops to refuel. Beside him is J. L. Norton, founder of the Norton motor cycle company. Fowler reached an average speed of 36.32 m.p.h. over the 158 miles of the old TT course. His record lap was taken at 42.91 m.p.h. and his petrol consumption was 87 miles per gallon. On the side of the machine is the Norton emblem.

cylinder engine, air-cooled, with each cylinder of 111.1 m.m. bore by 120.6 m.m. stroke. The frame was simple, consisting of one tube of enormous diameter running from the bottom socket lug, down under the motor crank chamber and up to the seat lug.

The tyres were 26 in. by 3½ in. and the weight of the machine was 360 lbs. Said one British report: 'This machine is to be ridden on the Parc des Princes track, which we hope will be sufficiently banked at the corners to prevent the plucky man who rides it from being killed.'

In 1903, Genty on his Griffon machine made the best time in speed trials at Nice, covering the mile from a standing start in 1 min. 16.95 secs, an average of 61.5 m.p.h.: blazing a trail on the other side of the world was American champion Oscar Hedstrom, as he flashed along the Daytona Beach in Florida.

On the Continent, motor cycling stormed ahead. France had no speed limits and riders were able to go to the nearest stretch of road and test their machines to the limit and as frequently as they wished. The sport flourished, rushing blindly ahead of its time, for motor-cycle races with no limitation on cylinder size resulted in engines with capacities in excess of 2 litres. These engines, mounted in two-wheel frames, produced some remarkable, unfortunate and occasionally frightening results. Crude and clumsy though some of these early efforts might now seem, this period of dash and daring was essential to the development of this pioneer sport.

The epic inter-city marathons for motorized vehicles had started in 1895, and by 1903 Bucquet, on a French-built Werner machine, had established a firm reputation. He had won the Paris-Vienna race and similar events and was leading yet again in the sensational Paris-Madrid event of 1903 when the race was abandoned at Bordeaux. By this time a number of spectators had been killed and injured by monster cars surging through great dust clouds as they charged over the pot-holed, primitive, spectator-lined roads. Forty-nine motor cycles took part. Bucquet completed the Paris-Bordeaux section of this ill-fated and uncompleted race, a distance of 341 miles, at an average speed of 38.12 m.p.h.

Competitors left Versailles in pairs at minute intervals and soon a struggle developed between Bucquet and Demester. Bucquet was the first to complete the 119 kilometres to Chateaudun, but even by this time the ultimate fate of the race was dimly visible. The motor cyclists found themselves mixed-up among the cars, which were beginning to give them a good deal of trouble, though the tourist cars were causing the greatest problem. The British rider A. C. Wright reported that he had to pull up to avoid running into

22 French rider Genty at Nice, the venue for many
record-breaking trials in the early 1900s. On this Griffon
machine he covered a mile from a standing
start in 1 min. 16.95 secs. (61.5 m.p.h.) in 1903.

23 Harry Collier with his Matchless at the 1912 TT; he finished
3rd in the Senior class at an average speed of 44.89 m.p.h.
24 Bordeaux, and the sad end of the Paris-Madrid race.

one car, which was drawn right across the road, and
the riders were increasingly concerned about safety
as spectators spread themselves over the course to such
a degree that many riders had to cut out and brake,
for fear of running them down.

Punctures and bursts, due to tyres being too light
for such a punishing test, were the cause of most of the
motor cycle retirements, but accidents involving motor
cycles were rare. The race was finally abandoned because
of the fatal accidents involving the big cars. As a spec-
tacle these roaring inter-city events over long distances
were sensational dramas which fired the imagination
and compelled the fanatical following of vast crowds.
Three million people are said to have lined the roads
for this Paris-Madrid race. As races they were searing,
brutish, frightening marathons — for spectators and
competitors alike. This final Paris-Madrid race was
an uncontrolled débâcle of immense magnitude and its
ignominious end at Bordeaux closed the door firmly
on the earliest chapter of motor-cycle sport.

After these marathon races, France continued to set
the pace and in 1904 the French Auto-Cycle Club, on
behalf of the Fédération Internationale des Clubs
Motorcyclistes, organized the first International Cup
Race, competed for by five nations — Austria, Denmark,
France, Germany and Great Britain. It was shabbily

conducted and ended in confusion and chaos. This
was a new form of racing, over a closed circuit, with
three riders competing from each country, and in spite
of its shameful mismanagement it anticipated our pre-
sent-day road race organization.

The British team took the rules seriously. Their three
riders, including Tom Silver, a long-distance specialist,
rode essentially British-built machines which weighed
no more than the 50 kgs (110 lbs) in accordance with
the regulations.

But the regulations appeared to be of the least consequence to many of the competitors, or indeed to the
organizers. Some riders rode machines different from
those on which they had been entered, or flagrantly
cheated by switching to machines which had not really
been produced in their own country; and it was all
part of the gamesmanship, it seemed, to delay the
opposition by showering the track with nails. The British
team, with a Continental vendetta being waged against
them, had so many punctures that they had to retire!
It was all a desperate shambles. The French annulled
the results and everybody tried to forget all about it.

The following year a second International Cup Race
was held. This was much better controlled and came
to be recognized as the first ever motor cycle race of
any consequence.

25 Maurice Fournier with his 22 h.p. racer 'The Monstrosity' of 1903; it was fitted with a special Buchet engine of more than two litres capacity, and it was generally considered that no rider would survive a race on it.

26 Tom Silver was one of three British riders competing in France's first International Cup Race in 1904, riding this British Quadrant Racer. Five nations took part in a race which ended in chaos.

27 Gamesmanship in the second International Cup Race, 1905—Cissac changing a wheel of his Peugeot, in complete defiance of the rules of the competition. Cissac's machine had a bore-stroke of 80 × 86 and was fitted with Dunlop tyres.

28 Victor C.V. Wondrick, the Austrian rider, on his rugged Laurin-Klement machine, in the Second International Cup Race. Wondrick is seen here at the finish at Dourdan with M. Klement and some spectators. He broke all previous records for the course at an average of 54.5 m.p.h.

Riders from France, Germany, Austria and England took part and knowledgeable observers at the beginning expected victory to go to France or Austria. Their riders were more accustomed to high speeds on the road and their machines were faster and more reliable for this kind of competition.

And so the first motor cycle race began. Demester, the favourite, led the way; Mueller of Germany went next, followed by Campbell of England and Toman of Austria. Twenty-four minutes after Demester, last off at number 12, was Wondrick.

Demester had a good first lap, uneventful, and he was riding well as he came round ahead of the field to start the second lap. Then his luck started to run out. He suffered a broken belt and punctures, so that Wondrick, whose tough machine had been built to withstand the severest stresses and who rode it superbly, with excellent cornering technique, moved into first place, leading Demester by 3 seconds. Toman, the favourite Austrian

rider, was now out of the race, having crashed on the first lap. In the third lap it clearly became a struggle between Wondrick and Demester and at the end of the third lap the Austrian was 1 minute 45 seconds ahead. The French ace was by no means demoralized and during the fourth lap he rode well and gained 19 seconds on his rival.

The race looked like building up into an exciting and keenly contested climax, but then a further puncture in the fourth lap put Demester out of the running. In spite of his persistent ill-luck, his final timing — just 7 minutes 47 seconds behind Wondrick — was exceptional. This was simply not Demester's day, however, for the final irony was his disqualification (for changing a wheel), which robbed the clever French rider of second place. Wondrick, riding a Laurin Klement two-cylinder machine, broke all previous records for the Dourdan course, covering 270 kilometres in 3 hours 5¼ minutes, an average speed of almost 54.5 m.p.h.

28

29 The start of the 1908 TT, showing part of the Triumph team, Jack Marshall (5), W. F. Newsome (6) and J. Slaughter (7). Triumph was placed first and third in the Singles category, Jack Marshall winning the race at an average 40.49 m.p.h. with a fastest lap of 42.48 m.p.h. Captain Sir R. K. Arbuthnot

was third. An incredible feature of the race was Jack Marshall's petrol consumption—117.6 miles per gallon.

30 The 1911 Senior TT, and Charlie Collier (Matchless) chases Boldt (NSU), during the first 'mountain course' TT. Collier was disqualified for refuelling en route, after finishing in second place.

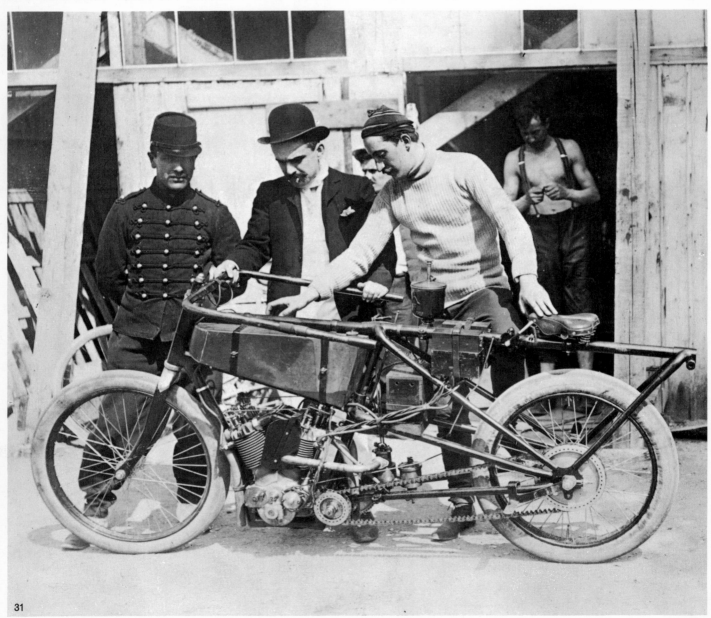

31 Fournier with his V-Four Clement at the Parc des Princes
track in Paris in July, 1903, just before the match
in which he beat Rigal (Griffon).

32 Rignold (Gt. Britain) making ready to leave Ablis
on his Lagonda at the start of the 1904 International Cup Race.
33 Demester, favourite in the first International Cup Race.
34 Joseph Giuppone on a 3½ h.p. Peugeot, 1909.

Demester rode a two-cylinder Griffon. The third, and only other rider to complete the course, was Joseph Giuppone, riding a French Peugeot, who took second place in spite of three punctures.

The International Cup Race, however, was acutely disliked by British riders who found their views completely aligned with those held by the British Auto-Cycle Club and between all the interested parties there emerged the desire and aim of a road race to be run under different rules, in Britain.

Among those who criticized the International Cup Races were the Collier brothers, Charles and Harry, whose early Matchless machines competed in these races. As designers they knew the illogicality of producing a suitable machine to the crippling weight limitation of 110 lbs. This restriction was inevitably producing big engines in light frames. Wheels were under-shod to meet the weight limitations, and the result was that machines were grossly overpowered for their weight. It was the organizers' insistence on maintaining this weight limitation which finally brought the extinction of the International Cup Race in 1906.

But already, motor-cycle sport was filled with excitement for a new venture. As the International Cup Race died in France, the idea was put forward for a British road race strictly for touring machines.

The idea was scotched by the authorities. Britain had a road speed limit and the Auto-Cycle Club was unable to obtain permission for certain public roads to be closed so that races could be run on them. Excitement sagged into despair until the ACC approached the Isle of Man authorities.

The eliminating trials to select a team to represent Britain in the International Cup in 1905 had been held on the Isle of Man, so what was more natural than to attempt to site the new road races there, once the mainland idea had faded. The Manx Government were

most cooperative. There was no speed limit on their roads and they had no objection to closing roads for the period of the races. It was perfect.

In such circumstances was born, in 1907, the greatest series of motor cycle races in the world — the glorious TTs. The sport was well on its way.

AN AMERICAN VICTORY AT BROOKLANDS

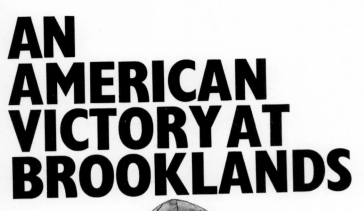

The magnificent Brooklands race track, 2.75 miles round, well-banked and situated near Weybridge in Surrey, was the scene of a great many races and record attempts during its exhilarating though comparatively short life-span. The best and most successful riders from all over the world went to race at Brooklands and one of the most stirring encounters ever to be staged there brought thrilling and sensational victory to America during the summer of 1911.

In a struggle for world supremacy, Charlie Collier, champion of England, met Jake de Rosier, USA, who only a week earlier had shattered three world records on his tough 994 c.c. Indian machine. Collier rode a Matchless, powered by a JAP engine of 985 c.c. The machines were in sharp contrast. The Indian, chain driven with 28-in. diameter wheels and thin tyres, looked lean and gaunt against the squat, rugged appearance of the British Matchless. Jake's engine was fitted with auxiliary exhaust ports drilled in the cylinder, the exhaust pipes were only 3 in. long and discharged straight into the open air. For the occasion, the American chose wide handlebars, his normal narrow handlebars being assessed as unsuitable on a bumpy track like

35   36

Brooklands. Collier's machine had no auxiliary exhausts, but was fitted with long exhaust pipes. 26 in. by 2 ¼ in. tyres had been fitted and the newly-introduced Matchless spring fork was used.

The two champions were to race three times over distances of two, five and ten laps, and as they appeared with their machines, which were wheeled out by their helpers, excitement round the track became intense.

Imagine the build-up of tension and expectancy. One observer wrote: 'At the start, Harry Collier wheeled his brother's machine down to the far end by the bridge over the Wey, and Garrett did the like with the Indian, while the two rivals walked down together, chatting to one another. The starter's car was also there, and presently it was seen that all three motors, i.e., the car and the two motor-bicycles, were coming nearer; faster and faster they went until, when the two competitors, were dead in line, down went the red flag in the car, and the race was begun. They crossed the line together with 'C.R.' perhaps a shade ahead. The exuberant feelings of the crowd gave vent in cheer after cheer, the bookmakers shouted louder than ever, and two

small dots flashed out of sight round the hill. A few seconds elapsed and then they came out from under the members' bridge, and were 100 yards beyond before the sound of their exhausts reached the listening ears of those at the fork.

'Jake was a couple of lengths behind, but began to close the gap quickly. They went out of sight again down the railway straight, and, when next viewed by the aero sheds, the Englishman was 10 yards ahead. They tore past the judge's box with Jake taking Collier's shelter, but, on leaving the big banking, the Indian got a wheel ahead for a few seconds. The Matchless, however, quickened up, and was in front at the aero sheds, and came into the straight first. Then came a most magnificent piece of riding by Jake, for he suddenly dashed away, and, before Charlie could quicken up, had got to the front.

Collier tucked his head down lower and made a final spurt, but it was too late, for, although he seemed to be catching up quickly, the Indian crossed the line first, though there was not daylight between them.'

Jake had won the first race by just one length at a speed of 80.59 m.p.h. Collier might have clinched victory for England, had he opened out going round the

last bend, but he allowed de Rosier to throttle up first and that was the key to victory.

In the second race, over five laps, Collier roared into the lead from the start and relentlessly surged forward in an exhibition of superb riding which kept him ahead of his rival. The crowd was stretched to fever-pitch. Jake de Rosier was seen to wobble badly, but he recovered. With his head well down, the great American racer was surging along in Collier's slipstream, the two of them speeding round the banked circuit at over 80 m.p.h. Faster still, their speed was now almost up into the 90s, but it became obvious that Jake was playing a shrewd game. He was letting 'C.R.' do the pacing, content for the moment to be pulled along in his wake. With three laps completed, Charlie Collier had kept England in the lead, but could he maintain his advantage? Then came a fantastic fourth lap. As the crowd craned forward to look for them coming round yet again, Collier was seen to be in the lead. There was no sign of the American. Charlie swept ahead to complete five laps, giving victory in the second race to England and levelling the score.

Jake, it was learned, had been forced to retire. His front tyre had burst while he had been travelling at

37

37 Four American aces with a formidable array of Indians on the beach at Daytona, December 1909. Left to right: Walter Goerke, Oscar Hedstrom, Robert Stubbs and A. G. Chapple. Hedstrom was American champion for some time.

38 Bardin and his de Dion tricycle in the 1897 Paris-Cabourg race.

39 Bucquet, winner of the Paris-Vienna race of 1902, on his French-built Werner. He also led the Paris-Madrid event of the following year until it was abandoned. These two pictures are in ceramic tiles, made in Paris in about 1910 by Gilardoni Fils, and are early Michelin publicity material.

40 Worters on his Excelsior at Brooklands, where he managed a 'stable' of racing stars.

41 The great Brooklands race track in Surrey in about 1924. The background to Jake de Rosier's sensational victory of 1911 over British champion Charlie Collier, it attracted top riders from all over the world. The hangers and the sweeping, high-banked circuit are clearly visible.

40

80 m.p.h.! At such speed it could easily have been a terrible disaster, but Jake was unscathed and prepared for the third and final race.

Now the tension was highest. One race to de Rosier. One race to Collier. The decider, over ten laps, met all expectations, and great excitement was generated.

The drama was heightened at the start, with the riders all set to go, when it was discovered that de Rosier's machine had one or two loose nuts and someone had to go off in search of a spanner. Then came a false start, after which it was discovered that one of the carbon brushes in Jake's magneto was broken. But the crowd's tension was only eased for a moment.

'But then, at last, they are away with Collier once more racing fractionally ahead of the American; round the first lap and into the second with Jake less than a length

41

42 D. R. Donovan, a tuning expert known as 'Wizard', with his Norton at Brooklands in 1913. In the background, a dramatic view of the famous Brooklands banking.

43 An imposing line-up at Brooklands during the 'golden era' of this track. For over thirty years, this magnificent concrete saucer was the scene of hundreds of races, successful record attempts and thousands of hours of testing by British machine manufacturers. Brooklands and the TT guaranteed Britain a place in the history of the motor cycle.

behind his English rival. It is de Rosier who crosses the line first on the next lap, but then Collier opens the throttle wide and, roaring down the railway straight, sweeps all of ten lengths ahead. It begins to look like a British victory and the jubilant fans shout for joy as Charlie completes the half mile at an average speed of 84.8 m.p.h.

'Jake rejects the possibility of defeat. As he races round the high banking for the fifth time, he is back in Charlie's slipstream. English eyes rivet on the two hunched figures with soft aviator-type helmets pulled tightly round their heads, and their hearts falter as Collier's Matchless begins to misfire. Charlie looks down, sees a high-tension wire adrift and, as the machine slows, he struggles to reconnect it to the plug. He does it, but in the meantime Jake is racing far ahead. When

42

43

44 W. Jones of Wrexham with the AJS on which he finished fourth in the 1914 Junior TT. This machine is now in the Mallory Park Motor Museum.

45 A modern speedway star, Barry Briggs, riding a vintage Norton at a recent Brighton Vintage Rally.

46 Brooklands on the day of the opening meet, 27 March, 1911.

47 A rider refuels during the 100 lap race at Brooklands on 30 June, 1910. The primitive pit facilities and the cavalier approach to the sport are well shown in this excellent picture.

48 A 1907 North London Garage racing motor cycle, belt driven, on which W. E. Cook won the first official motor cycle race at Brooklands in 1909. He did the flying kilometre at 75.92 m.p.h. The machine is now in the Montagu Motor Museum, Beaulieu, Hampshire.

49 F. W. Barnes in a Zenith leads the 'cycle-car and sidecar' race during the BMCRC sidecar race on 17 May, 1913. Note the basketwork sidecar.

he sees that Collier has run into trouble, the American sits up in the saddle and begins to take the race easily. But the redoubtable Charlie Collier is by no means out of the race, and the American has to get his head well down once more as he sees the Englishman pounding up behind him again.'

This is how one eye-witness described the dying moments of the race: 'When it came to the end of the seventh lap the little man in the airman's suit was but 20 secs ahead, and he was glancing behind him for quite long stretches to see where his opponent was. Looking round over his shoulder, without going out of his course, and at 80 miles an hour! What skill! What daring! In this eighth lap the champion of the home

side came up 2 seconds on the machine of the American, but receded .6 of a second on the penultimate circuit. And so, without making a mistake, Jake de Rosier won the third race, the final, and the prize money.'

The series had been a triumph for American technique. As English champion, Charlie Collier had been conditioned to racing to the front at the start of the race and staying there until the end. Jake de Rosier's pattern of riding was to stay close to his rival, nursing his machine along for most of the race, and then to make his supreme effort during the final stages: the astuteness of the rider, as well as his courage, strength and technical skill, was now becoming an important factor in the winning of races.

THE ROARING TWENTIES AND THIRTIES

The main centre of motor cycle sport during its fledge-ling years was the continent of Europe and, in particular, France, where long-distance road races and the very first road race over a closed circuit were held, though the United States, in 1911, made a dramatic impact. Their tough Indian machines, with two-speed, chain-drive transmissions, achieved sensational success, first at Brooklands through de Rosier's magnificent racing, and then in the TT races, when they became the first 'foreign' machines to prove their superiority over the punishing mountain circuit. They raced home to take the first three places in the Senior event.

By this time, however, the swing to Britain as the centre of motor cycle racing was already more than an indication, while interest on the Continent dropped away considerably. The United Kingdom's emergence as the leading nation coincided with what have since become recognized internationally as the sport's golden years, and was attributable directly to the establishment of the TT races on the Isle of Man and the opening of the Brooklands race circuit—both in 1907. These two significant developments gave British motor cycle racing the blood transfusion it needed and rapid progress was made in machine development and in racing skills during the following fifteen years. The TT races were to become the standard by which all other races were judged and with a cavalier kind of dash and buoyancy, Britain was destined to sweep to the top of international motor cycle sport.

The regulations for the TT races were simple, sensible and straight-forward. There was no limit to engine capacity or weight, but competitors were restricted to machines with a petrol consumption of 90 miles per gallon for singles and 75 for twins. Tool kits were obligatory (and were needed!), machines had to be fitted with working silencers, a proper saddle, mudguards and 2-in. diameter tyres. There was one other important condition: pedalling gear, to assist propulsion as and when necessary, was allowed in the first TT. The bikes were to avoid the mountain section of the course included in the TT races for motor cars, simply because it was not expected that they had the power — even

with pedalling gear — to climb Mount Snaefell! It has to be realised that in these early days, motor cycles were almost exclusively single-gear belt-driven models. The shorter course decided upon was approaching sixteen miles and had to be lapped ten times.

Riders were to be raced off in pairs. So history was made, on Tuesday, 28 May 1907. Eighteen single cylinder machines and seven twins competed. Included in the list of entries were names like Triumph, Matchless, Norton, and almost half of them completed the race. Charlie Collier on his Matchless won the single cylinder class. He completed the ten laps at an average

50 The exciting scene as riders prepare for the start of the Senior TT race in the Isle of Man, 1928. With plenty of talent there, both riders and machines, everything pointed to records being broken, but then the rain started... and continued. All thoughts of records disappeared as riders retired. Charlie Dodson went on to win one of the wettest TTs ever from G. E. Rowley.

51

53

32

51 A postwar Moto Guzzi Gambalunghino 250.
52 The greyhound silhouette of an NSU 350.
53 The oil-and-sawdust atmosphere which characterized the
early development days is well exemplified by this Norton depot.
Skill and foresight were also there, as the Norton name gained
a world-wide reputation through repeated victories.

54 A rider races past the Boy Scouts, placed in sight of each other so that obstructions could be signalled down the line to help to keep the 1910 TT route clear.

55 The Senior TT, 5 July, 1911. American Indian machines collect the first three places and his admirers lead the winner, O. C. Godfrey, away from the finish.

56 The machines are assembled for examination and sealing before the start of the 1911 Junior TT.

speed of 38.22 m.p.h. The twin-cylinder race was won by H. Rem Fowler on a Norton at an average speed of 36.22 m.p.h. The year 1907 was doubly significant in the history of British racing — and indeed throughout international motor cycle sport — because of the opening of the famous Brooklands race track. Now, for the first time, British riders had a realistic opportunity to test their machines and advance their development by running them to the very limit on this superb, banked circuit. Brooklands' first motor cycle race took place on 20 April 1908. Later that year other races were held and in a short time Brooklands became the regular home not only for races, but for testing new machines and modifications, and for record-breaking attempts.

World War I halted the developing tidal wave of interest and enthusiasm for the sport for five years, but then, in 1920, racing burst through once more, but this time with the enthusiastic backing of works teams and interested manufacturers. Through the twenties and thirties the golden boys of British racing dominated the world. Men such as Stanley Woods, Wal Handley, Alec Bennett, Jimmy Simpson, Graham Walker, Jimmy Guthrie, Freddie Frith and Harold Daniell raced to victory after victory to become legends in their own time. In this flood of interest and excitement significant events were taking place. Scrambling, point-to-point racing over rough terrain, was born, and in the late 1920s dirt-track racing left the apron-strings of its home country, Australia, to capture the imagination of Europe. In 1930 Joe Wright, in Ireland, set a new world motor cycle maximum-speed record at 150.5 m.p.h.

54

55

56

57 Crouched low, D. B. Bolton on a 3½ h.p. Rudge comes in close as he rounds Hairpin Corner in the Senior TT of 1912. Rudges did not enter an official team, but four private owners rode Rudge Multis. Indian machines, so outstandingly successful

the previous year, were unplaced. F. A. Applebee on a Scott was the winner. Haswell on a Triumph was second and H. Collier, third.

57

The French Grand Prix, the only event of any importance remaining on the Continent immediately prior to World War I, was revived in the 1920s and during this heyday of motor cycle racing it was joined by similar events in Belgium, Ireland, Italy, Holland, Germany and elsewhere to form the basis of the present grand-prix programme. British machines with British riders dominated these European circuits, and carrying the cluster of British riders to international reputations were machines which were to become equally famous — Sunbeam, AJS, Rudge, Velocette and, above all, Norton. They were to become virtually invincible, carrying off race after race. They scoved over 30 TT victories and, after the war, over 20 riders' and manufacturers' world championships. In the 1930s and for some time after the war, they swept from one victory to another both in England and abroad.

A quiet man, Joe Craig, was the genius behind the Norton miracle. He was a development engineer and racing chief of enormous talent and had the ability to recognize and select some of the best riders the world

has known. The famous single-cylinder Nortons were nurtured and developed by Craig with a feeling and finesse which was an inspiration to the entire industry. Joe Craig drifted into racing as a private owner competing in hill-climbs in Northern Ireland in 1921. He rode in the Ulster Grand Prix of 1925 and three years later joined the Norton team of riders, but he was always more interested in the back-room business. Recalled Joe: 'I can truthfully say that I never really enjoyed the riding in a race as much as the pleasure derived from prying into the reason as to how and why the machine worked. My primary interest was centred in developing or improving the breed, in being able eventually to have put on the starting line, by some means not seriously contemplated in those days, a machine which, suitably conducted, would be capable of setting a really cracking pace and, above all, be worthy of success.'

In 1929 Joe Craig retired from the Norton team and went home to Ballymena and at this point he was in danger of being lost to the racing game for good. But later that same year Norton's asked him if he would

58 Harry Daniell and a well-wisher on the Isle of Man at the 1933 TT. AJSs and Nortons were his machines.
59 Alec Bennett after winning the 1927 Senior TT on the first Camshaft Norton, with G. Albert and J. W. Shaw.
60 1935, and Freddie Frith (42) and R. Harris congratulate each other on Manx Grand Prix victories.
61 The lever-operated banking sidecar outfit which could be made to lean out with the cycle on a corner; it is driven here by Freddy Dixon, who used it to win the first sidecar TT in 1923 at an average speed of 53.15 m.p.h.

consider returning to England to take a much more active part in the development and running of their racing machines.

He accepted and immediately set to work. The Ulster Grand Prix was but a few weeks away and the Norton machines had been somewhat disappointing. Craig concentrated on improving reliability and was successful to such an extent that the two 500 c.c. Nortons entered in the Ulster finished second and third.

The founder of Nortons, James L. Norton, rode in early TT races and his love for the sport dictated a policy of support for racing which his successors were to follow after his death. In the following years Nortons reaped fantastic success and world-wide acclaim. From 1931 to 1939 Nortons won both the Junior and Senior TT no fewer than six times. They entered eighteen TT races and were ridden to victory in fourteen. It was a superlative record. Norton throughout these years maintained a firmly traditional approach to machine development and it was this which, eventually,

was to lead them from the racing scene after a glorious record spanning almost two decades.

There was a hint of things to come in 1935 when Stanley Woods won the Senior TT on an Italian Moto-Guzzi, but a more imminent threat was from Germany. The BMW concern in Munich began making motor cycles in 1923 as an off-shoot of their aircraft engine production and immediately their machines caused something of a sensation. In the late thirties the BMW twin-cylinder machines, supercharged and with telescopic front forks and rear springing, broke into the Norton dominance of the 500 c.c. class, winning many races on the Continent. The supercharged BMWs were undoubtedly faster than the Nortons and this additional power more than compensated for the Nortons' better handling. Nortons battled to retain their mastery, but the going was hard. Concentration on the 500 c.c. machines had meant neglect of the 350s, and Velocette stepped in to take the 1938 and 1939 Junior TTs.

In 1939, partly because of the international situation,

62 Alec Bennett pulls in to refuel his Norton in the 1924 Senior TT. Note the interested crowd, the primitive pits, and the ever-present Boy Scouts and corrugated iron sheeting. Bennett went on to win at an average speed of 61.64 m.p.h.

63 The AJS workshops prepare for the 1924 TT.

62

63

64 Two of the sport's greatest riders. Stanley Woods (left) congratulates Jimmy Guthrie after the latter had won the Junior TT of 1937. Guthrie, riding a Norton, completed the 264¼ miles in 3 hours, 7 minutes, 42 seconds at an average speed of 84.43 m.p.h. He also tied with Frith in establishing the fastest lap speed at 85.18 m.p.h.

65 1933 Senior TT winner Stanley Woods (29), with speed and lap records of 81.04 and 82.74 m.p.h. J. H. Simpson (15) was second and P. Hunt, third. All three rode Nortons, and Norton won the manufacturers' and club team prizes. Woods also won the Junior event that same year.

Nortons did not enter a works team in the TT and some cynics, witnessing the difficulties the Nortons were having on European circuits, suggested it might be more because of the fine performances being registered by the multi-cylinder BMWs and the supercharged four-cylinder Gileras. Norton claimed this had nothing to do with their withdrawal and added, later: 'A multi-cylinder supercharged machine obviously had distinct advantages over a naturally aspirated engine and we were ploughing a lone furrow with no Government backing, unlike manufacturers in the other countries.'

Norton proved their point after the war by re-entering racing, with a team which again dominated the scene for a time. The FIM's ban on superchargers facilitated this and, while the supercharger experts went back to their drawing boards, Norton brought out their original 1938 machines to score many successes in 1947 and 1948. As the war clouds were gathering however, it was to Germany that the motor cycle world looked, for Georg Meier, riding a BMW, won the Senior TT to make history by becoming the first, and so far the only, non-British rider to win that race on a non-British machine.

In what was to be the last Senior TT for eight years, the supercharged German BMWs ridden by Georg Meier and Jock West started favourites. At practice the German machines had powerfully demonstrated their superior speed on the straights and acceleration out of the corners. Meier and West had ridden them with power to spare, but still Frith, Daniell and Woods could not get near to the BMW timings. 51 machines started the race and Harold Daniell was first off, but his first lap timing was poor and he didn't figure on the leaderboard. Georg Meier was quick to show his ability and was soon 52 seconds up on Stanley Woods and Jock West, with Freddie Frith in fourth place. Meier increased his lead in the second lap and registered the fastest lap of the day at an average of 90.75 m.p.h. On the third lap the German went further ahead and then, in the fourth lap, came the only possible hint of a British revival. Frith moved up into third place to lead Stanley Woods by 28 seconds, but there was no holding Georg. He steadily increased his lead—2 minutes 7 seconds up in the fifth lap, 2 minutes in the sixth (because of a pit stop); 20 seconds more at the finish.

The TT continues to be the greatest road-race classic in the world and its sensations and thrills during its sixty years of existence are legion. Perhaps its astonishing progress is best exemplified in Mike Hailwood's 250 c.c. race victory in 1967. He shattered lap and race records at 104.5 m.p.h. and 103.07 m.p.h. and in doing so registered his tenth TT victory to equal the record of the great Stanley Woods.

66

THE ITALIANS DOMINATE

Sunday, 2 July 1950, and the nine-mile sweeping circuit at Spa in Belgium is bathed in brilliant sunshine as thousands of excited spectators anticipate the start of the 500 c.c. Grand Prix. Already thay have witnessed some great racing, first in the Junior class, which had been won by Bob Foster on a Velocette, and then in the sidecar event when Norton, through Eric Oliver, won from Ercole Frigerio on a Gilera. Keenly expectant they might well have been, but few could have realized that they were about to witness some of the most spectacular racing since the war, with a sensational bonus of records into the bargain.

The battle of the 'heavies' was on, between Italy and Great Britain: Gilera, MV and Guzzi ranged against Norton, Velocette and AJS. The air-cooled, four-cylinder Gileras of Carlo Bandirola, Nello Pagani and Umberto Masetti were known to be quick; but had the Italian factory overcome the problems of poor handling and low speed torque which had so far prejudiced their racing ambitions? It was remembered that, as far back

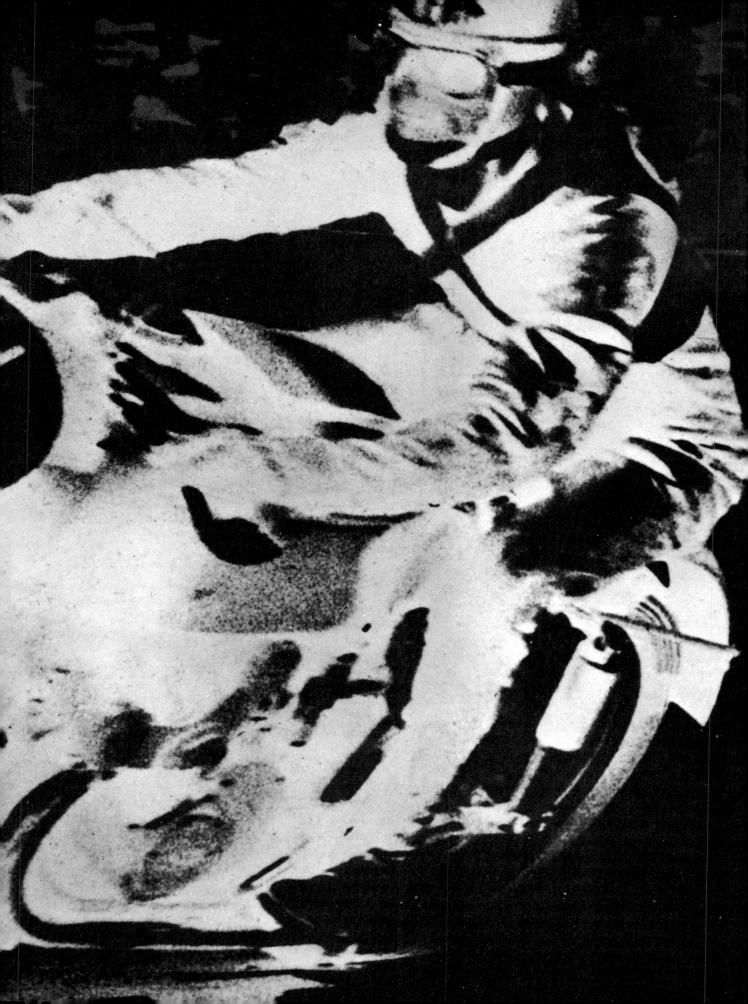

68 Italy and Britain do battle at the sweeping circuit at Spa during the Belgian Grand Prix of 1950. Geoff Duke tries hard to outpace Pagani's Gilera, but the Italian is determined to stay ahead, and winds up second behind Masetti.

69 1935 and the remarkable Stanley Woods does it again, winning the Senior and Lightweight TTs, but this time with Guzzi machinery. Here he is congratulated by Signor Guzzi and some spectators after the Lightweight victory.

as 1937 a Gilera machine had been fast enough to break the hour record when piloted by Piero Taruffi at an impressive 121.23 m.p.h. And a Gilera 4 won the 1939 Ulster GP, ridden by Serafini. On the other hand, the British machines had staked an early claim to serious consideration and in practice, Nortons, with Geoff Duke and Artie Bell aboard, had bettered the practice timings registered by the Gileras.

As the riders took their places on the starting grid with Geoff Duke (Norton), Les Graham (AJS), Masetti, Bandirola and Pagani (Gileras) in the front row, all looked set for a great race.

Engines snarled and roared, and the cluster of machines, their riders bent low, were already searing away from the grandstand. The pack clung together as the first shots in this battle for 500 c.c. superiority between Italy and Britain were fired. As they raced over the Eau Rouge Bridge, it was Italy first (Pagani) and Italy second (Bandirola); but Duke and Bell were upholding British prestige, riding well up among the leaders. Speeds were high, but riders braked hard to take the exceptionally tight La Source hairpin. Bandirola takes the corner well, accelerates and roars away from the hairpin in the lead; but Bell rockets his Norton ahead of the others and chases after the Italian in a tremendous challenge. After him are Pagani, Duke, Graham, and Masetti in sixth place. Comes the sweeping right-hander at Malmedy, then on to Masta, Stavelot, round and back down the other side; now skill is beginning to tell. Surging along towards the La Source hairpin once more, British riders tighten their grip on the race. Les Graham, down in sixth place at the end of the first lap, has ridden his AJS in spectacular style and now occupies second position behind Bandirola, with Bell a yard or two behind, in third position. Italy first, Britain holding second and third positions! But now a shattering upset for Britain. Bandirola brakes. Les Graham brakes too, but not quite early enough: his front wheel brushes the Gilera. The AJS slides out of control and Graham is flung clear, but suffers no serious injury. Artie Bell, travelling at about 100 m.p.h., is less fortunate. He tries unsuccessfully to steer clear of the spinning, riderless machine. The momentum carries Bell and the two machines crashing into the timing box and the Irish rider is severly hurt.

With the muted throb engine power building up to an exciting roar as the riders come in sight of the grandstand once more, Bandirola is still there is front, but now, with Graham and Bell out of the race, Geoff Duke is taking up the challenge in second place. Pagani is riding third and Masetti fourth. In the third lap Duke rides his Norton into the lead in a fine exhibition of

technique, but Bandirola stays close and during the next lap regains the lead. In the fifth lap the pattern of the race begins to emerge. Masetti moves to the front, followed by Bandirola, with Duke third and Pagani fourth. The leaders are setting a searing pace — Pagani, now in the lead at the seventh lap and the half way stage, is registering an average of 101.55 m.p.h. with Masetti, Duke and Ted Frend (AJS) all exceeding 100 m.p.h. There is little doubt that Duke is Britain's big hope now, and he seems to sense the responsibility. In the eighth lap he noses forward to take the lead and at an increasing speed, produces a scintillating display of riding which keeps him ahead of the field and thirty seconds in front at the end of the eleventh lap.

At this point a most astonishing coincidence seemed possible. Duke was riding as No. 28. Earlier in the day Bob Foster, riding as No. 28, had won the 350 c.c. event and then, remarkably, Eric Oliver, again No. 28, won the sidecar race.

Could Geoff Duke confound the cynics? He was still in the lead in the twelfth lap. About 105 miles of the 126-mile race had now been completed. Less than two laps to go and Duke was ahead. Then half way round lap 12, as he prepared to negotiate the Masta bends, he eased back the throttle, slowed down and stopped. Then slowly he rode dejectedly into the pits, a section of tread having been flung off his rear tyre. The British effort was spent. Frend rode hard and almost caught Pagani to take second place... but not quite. Umberto Masetti was the winner for Italy, with Pagani and then Frend. Duke notched the fastest lap at 103.89 m.p.h. and Masetti created a new road race record at an average speed of 101.18 m.p.h.

No-one doubts that Britain was robbed of victory by appalling misfortune, for Duke looked all set to win, but the result of the Belgian Grand Prix of 1950 was a symbol. It represented the forthcoming dominance of Italy in the 500 c.c. class and the beginning of the decline of British machines as a serious world challenge. Umberto Masetti was that year to go on to win the 500 c.c. individual world championship, though Geoff Duke ran him close, and in the next five years the Italian factories of Gilera and Moto-Guzzi were to blaze a glorious trail in road racing with victory upon victory on all the major European circuits. Gilera, and later MV, were invincible in the Senior events until 1966. The single-cylinder Nortons were outpaced and outclassed, and the firm disbanded its works team in 1955. The crippling costs of racing combined with the dwindling motor-cycle market in Italy forced the retirement in 1957 of Guzzi and Gilera, and the persistent MV were left a virtually empty field until the serious Jap-anese big-bike challenge.

But first came those glorious years between 1950 and 1957 when Gilera and Guzzi contributed one of the most spectacular chapters of motor cycle racing history. Guzzi had entered racing as early as 1920 and fifteen years later it was Britain's Stanley Woods who brought them immortality when he won both the Lightweight and Senior TTs on Guzzi machinery. For some six years after the war Guzzi dominated 250 c.c. races throughout the world and then won the manufacturers' world championship in 1953, their first year of 350 c.c. competition. Guzzi brought a new science to the development of motor-cycle machinery and the legendary wind tunnel which they built to test and develop streamlining is to this day talked of with reverence and awe, as is their engineer Giulio Carcano, the design genius who made it all possible. Throughout their distinguished history in the sport, Guzzi perfected the horizontal single-cylinder engine and their amazing versatility ranged from the famous 'single' to an amazing 'vee-eight'.

The name Gilera rings magically in the highest temples of the sport. This famous Italian factory had painstakingly developed their machinery from the mid-thirties and were about to mount a major offensive in the Senior class when war interrupted their ambitions. It seemed just and right that they should be on the scene once more in immediate post-war years, but it took time for them to break the persistent stranglehold which Norton were reluctant to yield in the late Forties.

Masetti's victory in the Belgian Grand Prix of 1950 was a pointer and for the next seven years Gilera provided wonderful displays and collected all the highest honours. Masetti, Duke and Libero Liberati, rode Gileras to win six riders' world championships in eight years, and victory in over thirty grand prix.

McIntyre joined the Gilera team in 1957 and in that same year at Monza turned in one of his greatest rides, on a Gilera 350, to break the one-hour record. His success with them, though brief, was explosive. He won both the Senior and Junior TT races that year and became the first rider to lap the Mountain Circuit on the Isle of Man in excess of 100 m.p.h. The Senior was an epic race, for not only did McIntyre, one of the really great riders whose career was destined to end so tragically in a fatal accident, raise the lap record to 101.12 m.p.h., but he managed to top 100 m.p.h. on three other laps.

British machines were challenged by a quartet from abroad in the form of Moto-Guzzi, Gilera, MV and BMW. No true comparison of the merits of all the four makes could be made. Generally, however, the

71

Guzzi 'vee eight' was recognised as potentially the fastest, but its reliability and handling were suspect. Both the Gilera and MV machines were more reliable, Gileras being superior from the point of view of handling. The reliability of the BMW was without question. As it turned out, Bob and his Gilera had a comfortable victory and the only scars of his record-breaking victory were fatigue and a cut on the forehead resulting from a stone which had spun up in his face from the rear wheel of another machine on the climb out of Union Mills on the fifth lap.

The Gilera, equally, showed little sign of stress. A report on how the race machines stripped revealed: 'The 3.50 inch-section rear tyre was little more than half worn, while the front tyre wear was even less. Both tyres were worn more on the right side than on the left. There was virtually no oil on the walls of the rear tyre, though a slight amount was trapped in the wheel rim. The power unit was clean externally and brake, clutch and chain settings were not in need of even minor adjustments.'

This showed how well within its potential the Gilera had been raced and McIntyre, never a rider to travel faster than was necessary to win, might well have broken the 100 m.p.h. lap by a considerably greater margin if it had been necessary for him to do so. This victory really confirmed the superiority of the four-cylinder design in the larger classes. But it was left to the Italian factory's home-bred rider Libero Liberati to ring down the curtain on Gilera's glorious reign. He became the 500 c.c. world champion riding a Gilera in 1957, the year the firm retired from racing, not so far to reappear.

The demise of Guzzi and Gilera left a huge gap in big-time road racing in the heavier classes which would have constituted a monumental disaster had it not been for one man — a human phenomenon, Count Domenico Agusta of Italy. His passionate interest in motor-cycle sport established the MV factory as a serious racing concern in 1950. The company, under the Count's father, was in the aircraft business, but, with the war over, other manufacture became necessary and it was largely

72

the Count's influence which brought them into two-wheeler production. MV's racing baptism soon after the war was inauspicious, but it was no secret in Italy that the Count's ultimate ambition was to win the 500 c.c. class. He cast envious eyes at the astounding success of the nearby Gilera factory and concentrated on producing a machine which would establish MV as a giant in world-wide road racing.

His first four-cylinder 500 c.c. machine fell short of the mark. Mainly the product of former Gilera designer Ing Remor, it had similarities to the Gilera, but with shaft final drive and torsion-bar suspension. It was a brave effort, more reliable than some experts might have anticipated, and it achieved moderate success.

The Count, his machine plans established, looked round for a top rider. Britain's Les Graham had won the world championship in 1949 on an AJS. The Count decided he wanted Graham: and the Count was the sort of man who generally seemed to get what he wanted. Graham signed for MV. Even with the Graham

skill the MV was not equal to the Gilera, and development work was forced ahead. By 1950 Gilera had virtually overcome the Norton dominance in the 500 c.c. world-championship competition, though Duke was to give the English factory a final fling by winning the 1951 title; but the breakthrough for which Count Agusta hoped was still some time hence.

In 1952 he had the consolation of seeing Cecil Sandford bring the 125 c.c. world title to MV, the first international success for the Italian factory, but in the 250 c.c. championship Guzzi continued to dominate; Geoff Duke kept the Norton flag flying in the 350 c.c. category, and it was Gilera back again in the 500 c.c. class to repeat their triumph of 1950.

Three years later, in 1955, MV were set for the long-awaited breakthrough. Unstinting investment, tenacity, passionate desire to see his machines the best in the world, painstaking development work—in 1955 these were signs that the Count was almost there. Not quite world supremo... but in a year or two?

73 Moto Guzzi's 500 'standard' of 1921.
74 By contrast, the Guzzi V-8 of 1957.
75 The MV stable at the 1956 TT.
76 The Guzzi wind tunnel.

A diminutive Italian with an almost Anglo-Saxon temperament, Carlo Ubbiali, secured MV Agusta's next success. Ubbiali's racing had started with Mondial and he stayed with them for three years, racing against the superiority of the German NSUs in the 125 c.c. class. He signed for MV in 1953 and two years later brought home the 125 c.c. world title. He repeated the success in 1956 and also captured the 250 c.c. championship. MV completed a year of sensational racing when John Surtees, after being signed to a long-term contract to race 350s and 500s for MV, collected the 500 c.c. world championship. With riders of the calibre of Surtees and Ubbiali it looked as if the MV concern had at last found the measure of Gilera in the 500 c.c. class, and Guzzi in the 350; and with the phenomenally successful German NSU factory now retiring from the 250 and 125 classes, all doors seemed to be opening. But *would* the machines stand up to the crucial test?

John Surtees had made no secret of his concern when he was approached by MV. He recalls: 'On the first trial I was greatly impressed by the engine's performance. The suspension seemed too soft, however, and had too much movement—a full six inches, I discovered.' Surtees' ideas and suggestions, and those of Les Graham earlier, resulted in modifications to the frame of the big four-cylinder MVs and improvements were also attempted in an effort to get more power. There were many

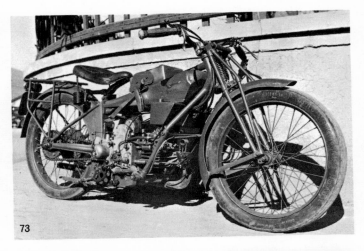

73

74

75

experiments with the suspension to get it to Surtees' liking. The handling of the MV at high speeds was not too good and Surtees said later that at speeds much in excess of 100 m.p.h. it required considerable physical strength to swing it round curves. But John Surtees was good for MV. The rider/owner relationship is not always an easy one, and with the confrontation of two strong personalities like Surtees and Count Agusta a clash of ideas might well have resulted. As a rider of outstanding skill, John Surtees knew what he wanted: on one occasion modifications were undertaken without his knowledge. The MV Fours had tended to 'ground' on corners and the angle of the front fork was altered in the hope that this would provide more ground clearance. No-one told Surtees, he claimed afterwards, and he crashed. His lack of knowledge of this modification, he asserted, could have been a cause of the spill, as the MV had felt light at the front. Thereafter Surtees insisted on it being definitely understood that no modifications or changes should be carried out on any of the machines he was to ride, without his knowledge. Communications improved after this episode.

One of the big speculations has been whether, had Gilera and Guzzi continued racing, MV would have been able to dominate the 350 and 500 c.c. competitions as they have done in recent years. For almost a decade the MV was unapproachable in the 500 c.c.

class, though it had little serious opposition in the period 1958-64, while in the 350 c.c. category the combination of Redman and Honda took over the world championship in 1962, breaking a four-year MV dominance. Certainly, the challenge which the two 'big Gs' could have mounted would have given Count Agusta a much stormier passage. Gilera and Guzzi disappeared from the circuits in 1957 for a self-imposed three-year retirement. They said they would be back in 1960 but so far only the Gileras have made a brief come-back. Sadly, they are still absent.

Meanwhile MV, in spite of a strong combined Honda/Hailwood assault in 1966 and 1967, continues powerfully in the 500 c.c. events and to say their record is outstanding is doing the ebullient Count Domenico Agusta a disservice. MVs have won the 500 c.c. riders' championship without interruption from 1958 through Surtees, Gary Hocking, Mike Hailwood and Giacomo Agostini. They captured the 350 c.c. world title from 1958 to 1961 inclusive, (since when they have been eclipsed by Honda), and most of the 250 and 125 c.c. titles from 1952 to 1960. Count Agusta has every reason to be satisfied with his decision to involve MV in international motor cycle racing.

Duelling is usually between riders, but not always. The time when machines perhaps were more important was 1963 when Gilera mounts of 1957 were brought

77 Britain's Geoff Duke riding a Gilera at the British Motor Cycle Racing Club meeting at Oulton Park, Cheshire, in 1956. After being Norton-mounted, Duke had big successes with the Italian factory.

78 One of the greatest motor cycle racers ever produced by Italy, Carlo Ubbiali, prepares for the 1953 Lightweight TT; riding an MV, he had to retire from the race.

77

78

79

79 John Surtees, who rode from success to success in races all over the world. At twenty-five he had already captured five world championships and six TTs. He rode Nortons until 1956, when he switched to MVs.

80 Gary Hocking, a favourite for the 1962 Senior TT, riding a practice lap over the course on his 500 c.c. MV Agusta. He won the Senior at 103.51 m.p.h. (average) and was second in the Junior event.

out from under dust covers following an enterprising move by former champion Geoffrey Duke.

Gilera had been absent from racing for six long years. In the meantime MV had seized the opportunity with outstanding success and in the 500 c.c. class had dominated the world. The sport needed a serious challenger... and looked back with nostalgia to the glorious days before Gilera's retirement from the racing scene.

The famous Italian factory was dogged in its determination to stay out of racing, though the machines which Geoff Duke and Reg Armstrong had ridden successfully in 1957 were still there in the Gilera factory. Duke persuaded the Italians to lend him the bikes, on two conditions: the machines must first be thoroughly tested; and the loan would be for one season only. Geoff Duke signed Derek Minter, one of the greatest short-circuits racers ever produced by Britain, and John Hartle, to race the Gileras and at Monza, during tests, both riders were clocking around 116 m.p.h. Minter, in spite of the machines' prolonged layoff, managed to hurl the Gilera round at over 118 m.p.h.—faster than a Gilera had ever before been raced at Monza.

Perhaps Duke's brainwave was not such a crack-pot scheme after all! Almost overnight, the 500 c.c. world championship was infused with a spirit and buoyancy which had been lacking for years. Here at last were Italian neighbours Gilera all set to do battle and mount a serious challenge to the might of MV. An epic clash between these two giants of motor cycle racing was anticipated with an almost uncontainable excitement. The whole motor cycling world waited for what was surely going to be the most exciting 500 c.c. championship in years.

At national meetings in Britain the return of Gilera brought out the crowds and Minter and Hartle raced the machines well. Hailwood, in the meantime, had signed for another season with MV.

At the international meeting at Imola in Italy, a crowd of 40,000 saw the opening battle. As the flag dropped, the MV with Hailwood aboard raced into the lead with Silvio Grassetti, on the second MV, just behind him. The two Gileras had started badly, but rapidly closed the gap. At the end of the first lap, both Minter and Hartle had been able to move ahead of the Italian Grassetti.

Hailwood was holding on the lead. In the fifth lap he still led Minter by some 400 yards, but by the end of the tenth lap, with fifteen laps still to go, Minter had fought to within inches of Mike's rear wheel. For two laps these two great riders battled and then Minter managed to edge the Gilera into the lead and immediately began to open the space. Minter raced on

to win, though four laps from the end it seemed doubtful. Said Derek: 'The machine developed gearbox trouble and every time I got revs on in 4th, it jumped out of gear.'

Gilera had certainly astounded the race game, for John Hartle managed to take second place. But for those who saw this as a Gilera revival, bitter disappointed was imminent. Minter crashed heavily at Brands a few weeks later and Geoffrey Duke had to find a replacement. There was disagreement between rider and sponsor; Hartle pranged one of the Gileras; and in the Ulster Grand Prix, Minter disappointed himself and his fans by doing no better than third.

In other events there were some fine non-classic duels between the MVs and the Gileras, with Hailwood and Minter as the chief protagonists. Towards the end of the season the two top riders met at Mallory Park in the 'Race of the Year' and Mike rode superbly to beat Derek by more than 30 seconds.

It had been a brave effort on Duke's part and although the challenge had been met and held off by MV, the racing proved what superb machines those 1957 Gileras were, although initial high hopes were never quite fulfilled.

49

81 The Honda team for the '66 TT; in T-shirts, Jim Redman,
Mike Hailwood, Stuart Graham, Luigi Taveri, team manager
Ikosan and Ralph Bryans.

81

THE JAPANESE TAKE THE LEAD

The 1960s began in a blaze of glory for Italy and MV. The famous Italian marque thundered to world titles in the 500, 350, 250 and 125 c.c. championships. It was a hat-trick all along the line, for MV had won those championships also in 1958 and 1959. Only in the side-car class, where Helmut Fath of West Germany continued the BMW success, was the name of MV absent. It was a remarkable display, deserving the greatest acclaim, but even its sheer invincibility was not sufficient to daunt the small yet almost obsessively determined Japanese. They had their sights set on world honours and even the phenomenal blast of power from MV was not permitted to shake their resolve.

The Honda factory carried out an intensive programme of development in their own country, but how their machines would compare with the might of Italy and other countries in world competition was open to speculation. Honda announced in 1956 their intention to race in Europe. Then, at the Isle of Man three years later, their double-overhead-camshaft parallel twins, conventionally designed, excited great admiration. This Japanese vanguard secured sixth, seventh and eleventh places in the 125 c.c. TT and gained the team prize— a remarkable achievement.

With Honda making a significant foothold on the world platform, and with Yamaha and Suzuki poised to launch themselves into international competition, the balance of power was shifting. The world-championship programme of 1960 provided the final grand slam for Europe. A year later, MV maintained their superiority in the 500 and 350 c.c. categories, but Honda, with Mike Hailwood riding a privately-entered machine, captured the 250 c.c. championship and Tom Phillis of Australia, also on a Honda, gained the 125 c.c. title.

Clearly, Japan had served notice on the world of motor cycle road racing. Just one year later, in 1962, MV were dramatically stripped of all except the 500 c.c. championship and the world was left gasping by Honda's explosive success. By this time that great rider from Rhodesia, Jim Redman, had signed for the Japanese factory and for them, in 1962, he secured both the 350 and 250 c.c. titles. Luigi Taveri, of Switzerland, won

82

the 125 c.c. championship on a Honda and the new 50 c.c. category was taken by West Germany's Ernst Degner, on a Japanese Suzuki.

Within the space of just twelve months Italy and Europe had been vanquished and Japan, even without further effort, had with one mighty season made one of the most sensational contributions ever to the world of motor-cycle sport. In races all round the world, Honda in 1962 demoralized and pulverized the most respected and revered opposition. Throughout the season Honda machines created one sensation after another. They established sixteen new race records in the twenty-five races in which they were entered. In the world championship Honda riders took positions 1,2,3, 4 and 6 in the 125 c.c. class; 1,2,4,6,7, and 8 in the 250 c.c. class; and 1,2 in the 350 c.c. class. As a crushing testimony to the world, Honda machines won all of the twenty-five races the team entered. Convincing though though these results were, Honda and Japan were merely setting the pattern for the years to come when a combined Honda, Yamaha and Suzuki onslaught captured most of the top honours for the Eastern World.

Jim Redman's views of the superb 350 c.c. Honda, though expressed with more than a tinge of emotion because of his close association with the Japanese factory, were nonetheless echoed by many: 'It's a breathtaking machine to race and one that seems impossible to break. When you let it go really hard you feel as if you have been flung from a catapult. You have to hang on tightly in case you get thrown back over the sad-

83

dle. Of all the bikes I have ridden, the three-fifty is the one
I have admired most. I have seldom been troubled by
rivals because of its tremendous speed, acceleration and
unwavering consistency'. Redman maintained, perhaps optimistically, that the 350 c.c. Honda was such
a magnificent machine that had it been bored out to
351 c.c. it would have given Mike Hailwood's unbeatab-
le MV a strong challenge! The skilful Rhodesian rider
captured the 350 c.c. world title for Honda and Japan
in 1963, '64 and '65, after which Hailwood continued
the tradition in 1966 and '67. In the 250 c.c. category
it was Honda and Redman again in 1963, Phil Read and
Yamaha in 1964 and 1965, Hailwood and Honda in
1966/67. Japan also dominated the ultra-lightweight
classes. In the 125 c.c. class it was Suzuki ('63), Honda
('64), Suzuki ('65), Honda ('66), and Yamaha ('67).
In the 50 c.c. class Suzuki, Suzuki, Honda, Suzuki and
Suzuki. Yamaha first appeared, internationally, in 1960,
but it took them time to make an impression. In 1962
their 250 air-cooled twin was perhaps the fastest machine in its class and in the TT Fumio Ito rode second
to Jim Redman, after Tony Godfrey had led before
crashing. The acquisition of Phil Read and later Bill
Ivy bolstered the Yamaha effort and provided the free-
spending Japanese factory with riders of the skill and
capability that are essential for major wins. Read quickly settled to the Yamaha twin, winning the French
Grand Prix in 1964 and then going on to collect the
world championship. The following year, now on a
water-cooled twin, Read won the 125 c.c. TT. Later,

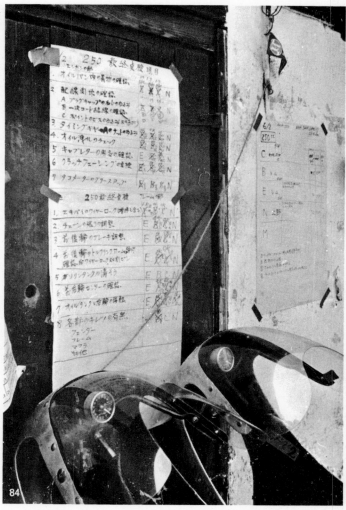

53

86 The Honda stable being prepared for practice in the 1959 TT; on this, their first appearance, they gained the 125 c.c. team prize.

87 The start of the 1962 50 c.c. TT; on Hondas are Shimazaki (5), Robb (8) and Taveri (10); Anscheidt (6) rides a Kreidler and Ito (12) a Suzuki. The winner was Degner on a Suzuki, Taveri was second and Robb third on a Honda.

86

87

88

Yamaha introduced the water-cooled, two stroke vee-four and a four-cylinder 125.

Some vintage road racing of the highest order was produced during the summer of 1964. By this time Mike Hailwood and MV so dominated the 500 c.c. class that much of its guts had gone. Mike, repeatedly, had only the clock and previous personal bests to beat. Though much more seriously challenged, Jim Redman on the Honda was firmly established at the head of the 350s; but in the lightweight class? That was a very different matter and the racing enthusiasts were not slow to recognise an interesting and exciting situation when they saw one.

Yamaha, in the 250 c.c. class, started the season determined to capture the title and with Phil Read astride the highly potent machine, their challenge was taken seriously, not least of all by Honda and Jim Redman, who were equally determined to retain the title. Earlier Honda had dominated, but by 1964 Suzuki and Yamaha had produced machines faster and more reliable than the Hondas.

The contest became keen when Phil Read won his first classic race at Clermont Ferrand. Read and Redman diced for half the race, but then the Honda went on to two cylinders and Redman had to retire. The Read-Redman duel continued ever keener as the classic programme unfolded and no-one experienced the tensions more than the riders themselves. Redman captures the tension of this personal battle in his description of the Belgian Grand Prix at Spa:

'He (Read) came like the wind. He zoomed by and I tucked in behind him. But I kept slightly to one side of his slipstream, knowing from experience that all two strokes have a heart-stopping habit of seizing in full flight. Phil was riding in the usual two-stroke rider's style, with one hand poised over the clutch ready to squeeze it in at the first signs of seizing. Then I saw a puff of smoke from one of his exhaust pipes and instantly I sensed his engine would lock. I started to swerve out of his slipstream just as we entered the full-bore 140-miles-an-hour 'Masta S' bend. As I swerved, Phil sat bolt upright and snatched the clutch in. His machine snaked but he stayed on.'

The Monza Grand Prix in Italy really decided the

89 Phil Read being congratulated by his wife and baby after winning the 1965 Lightweight TT. On the right, Taveri.

90 Jim Redman moving off from the pits: Francorchamps, 1966.

91 The 4-cylinder Yamaha about to make its European debut at Monza in 1965.

92 A mechanic's-eye-view of the 350 c.c. Honda 4-cylinder power unit (1963 model).

93 The Suzuki team for the 1963 TT, including H. Anderson (4), B. Schneider (1), and E. Degner (5).

94 1965 50 c.c. International TT; Taveri takes a corner.

championship in Yamaha's favour. By this time the war of nerves had built up to an almost unbearable level. Read was in front with more points and Redman had to win this vital race to stay in the running. The Honda camp mounted a huge psychological campaign against Read and Yamaha. They had been secretly developing a six-cylinder 250 c.c. back in Japan and decided, a little prematurely perhaps, to unveil it for Monza. Speculation and tension rose as the Honda was kept under dust-covers. Although it was well hidden and well guarded, two of its exhausts were removed to disguise it as a four-cylinder. When it emerged for practice as a full-blown six-cylinder the reaction was sensational.

Even so the battle of nerves was fully maintained by Honda. Redman kept the bike well within limits during practice and it was instantly covered again when it was wheeled in afterwards. As everybody clamoured for more details and information, Honda kept tight-lipped. Read and Yamaha might have been forgiven if they had departed the scene then!

The start of the race could only have added to Phil Read's despair. The Honda rocketed into the lead and, Redman maintained, using 1,000 revs under the maximum 17,000, was three seconds up at the end of the first lap. The Rhodesian had to win this race and the next and last grand prix in Japan to take the title. It was a tough job, but he'd made a great start and looked like zooming well ahead of the Yamaha. But then the Honda began to lose power and Redman had to race it on no more than three-quarter throttle. The machine's performance deteriorated and by the end of the race it was limping badly. Read had come up strongly on the third lap and eventually went on to win, and although he lost to the big Honda six in Japan, he had already secured the championship.

So far as is known at the time of writing, neither Yamaha or Suzuki have ever had ambitions to produce a world beating 500 c.c. machine, but Honda made no secret of their aspirations in this class. In a sensational move they signed Mike Hailwood from MV at the end of 1965 and he contested the senior championship in 1966 and again in 1967, but was thwarted in the contest for the rider title on both occasions, ironically enough, by MV and the great Italian rider Giacomo Agostini. Honda's design deficiencies, too much weight, bad handling and faulty gearbox were beyond even Hailwood!

For a time they were team-mates: then they became arch rivals. Between them Giacomo Agostini and Mike Hailwood have produced some of the most thrilling and spectacular duelling in contemporary road racing.

When Hailwood left the Italian factory for Honda

94

95 The Dutch TT, 1968; H. G. Anscheidt on his Suzuki.
96 Dave Simmonds at speed on a Kawasaki 250 in the Belgian Grand Prix, 1966.
97 Phil Read (1) and Bill Ivy (2) heel their 250 c.c. Yamahas hard over for a bend in the 1968 Dutch TT.

Three great duels: 98 Agostini and Hailwood playing cat and mouse at Assen 1967. Hailwood (2) eventually won by 5 seconds and created a new lap record.

99 Hailwood seems almost to be apologizing to Agostini after defeating him in the 1967 350 c.c. Junior TT. Small consolation for Agostini—Hailwood has broken the lap, race and absolute course records.

at the end of the 1965 season, he had dominated international 500 c.c. racing and had been world champion four times. With the giant resources of the Japanese factory to support him, Mike appeared to take on an even greater invincibility.

Agostini, who until Mike's departure had been second string to Hailwood—and something of a novice second string at that—had other ideas. Calmly, with great courage and skill and with the extra reliability of a larger version of the three-cylinder 350 c.c. MV, he refused to be intimidated by the Hailwood legend, which had now the additional backing of the massive Honda organisation. Against most predictions, Agostini retained the world title for MV in 1966 and, rubbing salt into Mike's already painful wound, repeated his success the following year. That year of 1967 must have been one of the most bitterly disappointing in Hailwood's entire racing career. His riding was as good as ever, but machine troubles persisted. In the West German Grand Prix he was holding a comfortable lead when the four-cylinder Honda smashed a crankshaft. At the Isle of Man that same year, these two staunch rivals rode one of the most remarkable races seen on the Island. Agostini swept into the lead and was in front for most of the race, while Hailwood struggled with a loose twist-grip. Then Giacomo, with little more than a lap to go, snapped his rear chain.

The duelling was resumed at the Dutch TT at Assen and before a stupendous crowd of 150,000, Hailwood rode a magnificent race. He kept close to Agostini for most of the time and then surged ahead to win. It was a tremendous effort which put Mike into a state of almost complete exhaustion. He almost fell off his ma-

100 Phil Read leads Bill Ivy in the epic 250 c.c. race at Mallory Park in June 1966.

chine at the end, and the presentation had to be delayed a few moments while he regained sufficient energy to climb the steps of the rostrum.

At Belgium, on the sweeping Spa circuit, Agostini was more than a match for Mike, though once again Hailwood had trouble with the Honda: and it was machine trouble yet again in East Germany, in spite of strong attempts by the Japanese mechanics to right things, which frustrated and disheartened Hailwood. His gearbox broke!

Agostini at this stage was ahead in the championship race by three victories to two. Hailwood won in Czechoslovakia, but Agostini moved ahead again in Finland after Mike crashed in the rain. At the Ulster Grand Prix it was the turn of the MV to have machine trouble and Mike levelled the score.

Monza, where Hailwood's hopes had foundered in 1966, was again to decide the championship for 1967: Mike moved away to a tremendous start and was solidly out-pacing Agostini, and in so doing beat the previous lap record by 3 m.p.h. Then, with just three laps to go, Mike became the victim of misfortune yet again: the Honda stuck in sixth gear. Agostini went on to win and to become World Champion yet again.

During the championship battle, perhaps the greatest excitement was amid the thrilling atmosphere of Assen, in Holland. This was a triple-win day for Mike, who outpaced everyone to be first man home in the 250, 350 and 500 c.c. classes. In the first and second events, Hailwood rode to easy victories on his six-cylinder Hondas, shattering the 250 c.c. lap record with a speed in excess of 91 m.p.h.

During practice for the 500 c.c. event, Hailwood had

100

101 Lunchtime conversation-piece, with pieces of Honda; Barcelona 1967.

102 Hockenheim, 1967; Hailwood's machine causes some puzzlement.

101

102

103

been fractionally faster than Agostini, but in spite of this, Agostini was hotly tipped to take the race following his victory in the TT. There was great excitement and tension as the two riders started well and raced away together.

The first break came from the Italian who, using the better lower-gear power of the MV well, edged forward and was in the lead at the end of lap I. Mike was close behind and was determined not to let Agostini go. As one report stated: 'Mike seemed content to play cat and mouse, easing up alongside the MV now and again.'

For nine thrilling laps Agostini 'towed' Mike, but then Hailwood demonstrated his tactical skill. As the two aces were lapping a bunch of riders, Mike outbraked Agostini as they went into a slow corner, and once he had his front wheel just fractionally ahead at last, he was determined to stay in the lead.

He pushed his lead to a hundred yards with some difficulty, but then began to pull away strongly. At one point he was leading by 17 seconds and finally won by 5 seconds, after creating a new lap record of 92.96 m.p.h.

Agostini took his revenge the next month when, in East Germany, he twice beat the British star. In the 350 c.c. event there was a great duel for more than half of the 18-lap race, Mike and Agostini swopping places regularly. In the ninth lap Agostini was held back by lapped riders and to the rising excitement of the 200,000 crowd, Mike pulled ahead. But the Italian wasn't having any of it. On the next lap he was right there with Hailwood again, but then Mike's bike faltered and petered out.

In the 500 c.c. event it was the MV off first again and over the first 200 yards to the first bend it was 20 yards up on the more sluggish Honda. On this occasion Mike was never able to make a serious challenge. His machine lasted only five laps and Hailwood's retirement left Agostini an open race. Even so, Agostini didn't make it. He already raced a record lap of 107.77 m.p.h. and was scorching downhill at 120 m.p.h. with little more than a lap to go, when he crashed and the MV was completely wrecked.

Both riders are a joy to watch at full throttle, and Hailwood's and Agostini's names have dominated the racing scene in the big-bike class in recent years. There is mutual admiration, in spite of arch-rivalry, and a great display of riding is assured whenever they meet. Ago's regular, handsome features and captivating smile make him a favourite with girl enthusiasts in most countries and he has a great following of fans like any celebrity in the entertainment world.

103 Honda mechanics cluster round Jim Redman in the
pits (1966).
104 Assembling a Honda from scratch; Francorchamps 1967.
105 Mike Duff on the Yamaha at Francorchamps in 1964.

104

105

CHAMPIONS ROUND THE WORLD

KEITH CAMPBELL

In 1957 the 350 c.c. world champion was an Australian, Keith Campbell, riding an Italian Guzzi machine. It is the only occasion an Australian has achieved 'world' status, but the victory, sadly, constituted a swan song for the famous Italian factory, whose name was not again to appear in the world championship charts.

Campbell was by no means a great stylist. He had plenty of dash and courage and although maintaining that he rode within his limits, he would also admit to riding flat out from start to finish. Without ballyhoo, with little experience, unknown, Keith Campbell arrived in Britain from Melbourne with a joke and a smile, but with the determination and singleness of purpose necessary for success. He was determined to be a road race champion and succeeded after nine years. This may suggest a long term plan, carefully and painstakingly executed, but Campbell's temperament was alien to this kind of calculated approach. He learned his craft by trial and error and with a vigorous Australian common sense, took his objectives one by one — letting the future look after itself. His early riding in Australia was on a 498 c.c. AJS. Then came a stab at scrambling, but in spite of two wins and a third place in three successive races, the lure of road racing was too great.

He changed his AJS for a 348 c.c. Velocette and made his own cams, using a simple bench-grinder. This was hardly a success, because the blow-back through the carburettor resulted in considerable lost power. But Keith Campbell was learning the business—and learning the hard way. In 1951 he entered the Junior Manx Grand Prix on his first trip to Europe. At half way he was in third position, but at the left hander before the Verandah he showed insufficient respect and paid the price with a broken thumb and a lacerated face. A year later he finished sixth in the Junior race of the Manx and, short of the fare that would take him home, went to work for Nortons where he met and later teamed with Gordon Laing on a number of European outings. A this time it could hardly be said that Keith was setting the racing world alight, but with two short-stroke Nortons at the beginning of 1954, the determined and uninhibited Aussie set out once again to conquer the European scene. Was this to be a final effort? Certainly, money was short—so short that he rode in the Belgian Grand Prix in spite of the fact that his left hand was in plaster following a spill during practice for the TTs.

This was a crucial time in Campbell's career. He did well to finish fifth in the 500 c.c. Belgian Grand Prix. Then, following a double victory at Vesoul, he went home to win the South Australian 350 c.c. championship. His European form in 1955 was sufficiently outstanding to bring him increasing attention and after

another impressive series of victories he signed for Guzzi in the autumn of 1956. Keith Campbell's cussed determination helped his success in the keenly competitive world of motor-cycle road racing. He displayed this character-line early in life when he shunned parental advice by quitting his engineering studies and again when he brushed aside the security of an apprenticeship to earn sufficient money for his fare to England. Without that determination, later in life, Campbell would have found it hard to ride the setbacks and frustrations of international road racing. In his first race for Guzzi he up-ended factory plans in typical style. He was lent a machine for the 350 c.c. race at Senigallia in Italy and the plan was that he should be in open competition with Guzzi team-mates Ken Kavanagh and Dickie Dale for the first six laps only, and then the three riders would maintain their positions. After a poor start owing to his unfamiliarity with coil ignition (he forgot to switch on!) he rushed through the field, passed Kavanagh on lap 4 to take the lead and then raced on to win. Guzzi knew then, if not before, that they had in Keith Campbell a character as well as a rider of extraordinary talent and they quickly signed him for the 1956 season. How sensationally he vindicated their confidence in him is now told by the record books.

It took Keith Campbell nine years to secure a works contract. It was cruel injustice that he had held it for such a short time when Guzzi announced their retirement from the racing scene.

107

66

WERNER HAAS

108

109

110

In 1956 Werner Haas died in an air crash. To the outside world the accident evoked the same kind of distant sympathy given to any similar tragedy. To motor cycling folk the news was received with a deep sense of personal shock. The memories came crowding back—memories of a curly-haired, happy-go-lucky genius on a racing motor cycle who just four years earlier had established an undeniable reputation as the greatest rider ever to come from Germany.

The reign of Werner Haas in the world of motor cycle racing was short but sensational. He joined the German NSU concern in 1952 and in that same year his neat, brilliant riding shocked the Italian Mondial organisation, for he beat them into first place in the 125 c.c. German Grand Prix; Mondial in the 125 c.c. class and Guzzi in the 250 c.c. had a sound grip on world honours at this time. The years 1953-4 were glorious times for Werner Haas and the German manufacturer. Although NSU had given support to racing and had developed supercharged 350 and 500 c.c. twins before the 1939-45 war, they had not been successful in post-war years. In 1950 they had contested the 500 class with a four-cylinder machine with atmospheric induction—superchargers by this time being no longer permitted: but the challenge slumped and NSU had therefore decided to concentrate on the 125 and 250 c.c. classes.

Haas rode in the TT races in both 1953 and '54 on NSU machinery, but the Island by no means provided his most glorious successes. In 1953 he placed second in the 125 c.c. and 250 c.c. categories and a year later he had to retire in the 125 c.c. event. He well made up for this disappointment in 1954, however, by winning the 250 c.c. race and recording the fastest lap at 91.22 m.p.h.

For two years Werner Haas raced their brilliant lightweight machines to outstanding success. In these two years he won the classic events and three world championships! In 1953 he became world champion in both the 125 and 250 c.c. classes, 250 c.c. world champion again in 1954. He was Germany's first and only double champion.

Shortly after these two years of outstanding performance by NSU and Werner Haas, the Neckarsum factory decided to quit racing. It would have been to the benefit and advantage of the sport for Werner to continue, but with his own successes having been so indivisible from NSU, he too decided to retire.

His meteoric rise to international recognition and his brilliant success was at an end. A year later came that fateful crash and the deeds of Werner Haas were left as a memorial to one of the greatest racing motor cyclists Germany has ever produced.

MIKE HAILWOOD

111 Flower-power Hailwood.
112 Hailwood and Honda at Brands Hatch.

Comparisons between generations in motor-cycle sport are difficult if not impossible to make. By what yardstick can the skill of Jimmy Guthrie, for instance, be measured against the skill of John Surtees? Machinery, technique, competition, opportunity—all had varied enormously in the intervening years. On one point, however, observers seem to find general agreement: that in recent times Mike Hailwood emerges as *the* most outstanding rider of his generation.

At seventeen Mike Hailwood showed promise in his first race and only a year later rode third, seventh, twelfth and thirteenth in the four solo classes in the Isle of Man TT—a remarkable record achievement. While still only eighteen, he won three out of the four ACU Road Racing Stars and notched sixty 'firsts' at race circuits throughout the United Kingdom. At twenty he became the youngest works rider and in 1961 captured his first world championship, the 250 c.c. on a Honda. That same year he also won the 125 c.c. and 250 c.c. TTs on Honda machines and the Senior on a Norton. In 1962 he signed for the Italian MV concern and immediately continued the MV tradition set by John Surtees, and then Gary Hocking, by taking the 500 c.c. world championship. Between 1962 and 1965 Hailwood was supreme in the 500 c.c. class, winning race after race, setting up scores of records and gaining the world championship continuously for MV. He also rode frequently and with success in other classes. For sheer number of wins, his record is supreme.

In impact value, Mike Hailwood has a stature unrivalled throughout the sport. His prosperous background, the international backcloth against which he performed, the jet-set, playboy image exemplified by the London bachelor flat and high-powered sports cars have added a lustre to a sport which had not been previously noted for its glamour or sophistication. Being the son of a wealthy father obviously brought him untold opportunities, but also an 'it's easy for you' reputation which was not easy to live with. Living down, or living with, the golden-boy image meant that Mike Hailwood had to underwrite his talent heavily to convince the world of his prowess.

On this there can be no doubt. As early as 1960, when Hailwood was only twenty and had but three years racing experience behind him, that noted British authority Murray Walker predicted: 'Before him lies the prospect of becoming the most successful rider in the history of motor-cycle racing.' That prospect became an indisputable fact.

In the 500 c.c. class he has repeatedly annihilated the opposition. Some would argue that the MV machinery which he rode was so far ahead of any rival to make such rivalry almost superfluous, and many less fortunate riders have openly pleaded for the miracle which would give them the chance to race against Mike with similar power. Speculation and conjecture are interesting, but the fact is that Mike Hailwood has been the most outstanding rider, perhaps, of all time.

After a spectacular career with MV, Hailwood signed for Honda for a high, though undisclosed, fee. There can have been little doubt that, with MV, Mike Hailwood was the world's highest-paid rider. Once he signed for Honda there can have been no doubt whatsoever. Mike was now back on machinery which had given him his first international successes. He set himself a full programme, contesting the 500, 350 and 250 c.c. classes against the world's toughest opposition. In the 1966 world road-racing championships he secured the 250 and 350 titles for Honda and also rode home in the 250 and 500 TTs. The 500 c.c. world championship, however, eluded him in 1966 and again in 1967, the title on both occasions going to Giacomo Agostini riding the MV.

Hailwood has produced countless scintillating performances, but one remembered perhaps above all others was the 1965 Senior TT when, in rain and sleet, he crashed while in the lead. His machine was damaged and he was shaken, but he remounted and in spite of a gradually failing engine, finished the course to win.

A writer on motor sport, commenting on the lack of colourful personalities in the car world, cited Hailwood as an example for the four-wheel boys to follow. Hailwood goes out of his way to have a good time, even to turning out in full Flower-Power kit at Snetterton.

This carefree clowning is part of the Hailwood legend —as essential to the good-time life of Mike the Bike as the succession of victories on the circuits the world over.

111

113 Baby-face Bryans with bouquet.
114 Ralph Bryans, head well down, at Clermont Ferrand.

RALPH BRYANS

Ralph Bryans is not exceptionally small, but he can tuck his 5 ft 8 in. frame neatly on to a racing machine with the best. For anyone in doubt, Ralph can catalogue convincing evidence, including a 50 c.c. world championship (no less!) in 1965. His big opportunity came in 1963 when Bultaco and Honda were quick to spot the Bryans potential. The previous year he had concentrated on racing in Ireland, winning the Cookstown 100 and securing third place in the North West 200. At a couple of meetings in Spain in October 1963, Ralph rode Bultacos in what were obviously test rides and afterwards signed for them. Jim Redman had also been impressed with Bryan's riding and recommended him as a possible works rider to Honda. When the Japanese factory made a definite offer just a couple of months after the Bultaco signing, Ralph found himself in the happy though unusual position of being able to make a choice between two attractive futures. The Honda opportunity and potential was the greater and when Bultaco heard of the Japanese factory's offer, they sportingly withdrew.

In his first year with Honda Bryans won four of the big races—the Dutch TT, the Belgian, West German and Japanese grands prix—and finished an astonishing second behind Hugh Anderson in the World Championship. This was a sensational debut, for at the start of the season the only classic circuits he knew at all were at Ulster and the Isle of Man. He rode skilfully and intelligently and his sensible approach to racing was observed in an interview: 'Go fast, just because I'm in a works team? I only run when I know where the road goes,' he said. During 1965 there was no-one to match Ralph Bryans in the 50 c.c. class and he completed a year of brilliant riding by securing the world crown, just six years after first entering the sport. Trials, scrambling, grass track events—all held interest and excitement for the teenage Bryans in the early days. Then in 1962 road racing monopolized his ambitions—an early flavour of success still tasting sweet from a 1960 victory in the 200 c.c. Irish Championship and he was soon to make an international reputation.

There is more than a mild touch of the spectacular about the Ralph Bryans story. He started running a bike in 1950 as a sixteen year old apprentice earning only £3 10s. in a week, and in doing so got close to the poverty line. He got the chance to race for the first time, deputizing for a friend in the Tandragee 100. He won the 200 c.c. class on a 197 c.c. Ambassador Villiers—a most remarkable achievement! Mounted on a Norton he finished second on handicap in the Skerries 100 of 1961 and a year later he collected ninth place in the 350 c.c. Ulster Grand Prix.

GIACOMO AGOSTINI

Think of Italy and motor cycle racing and you think immediately of one man: Giacomo Agostini. The handsome Italian has established such a solid international reputation in the 500 c.c. class in such a short time that it is hard to realize that prior to joining the MV team for the 1965 season, he had raced nothing bigger than 250 c.c. machines. His big-bike debut was sensational. At the end of the first season, and riding as team-mate to Mike Hailwood, he finished runner-up to the British rider in the 500 c.c. world championship and only a mechanical failure in the Japanese Grand Prix robbed him of the 350 c.c. title. In less than a year he had rocketed from obscurity to world status. More Agostini magic, however, was to come. His success the very next year was devastating. During the close season Hailwood had moved to the Honda camp and the former team-mates became keen rivals. The 500 c.c. world championship was a duel between Mike and Agostini from the start. This pair captured and held the attention throughout the season and the Italian, racing in his own country at Monza, secured the title in the final 500 c.c. race of the series.

Nothing could stop the Agostini onslaught. No-one could match it. Earlier in the season he had won the 350 c.c. TT on the Isle of Man and he went on to finish the year in a blaze of glory with shattering performances at a number of short-circuit meetings in England. In September he collected the 1,000-guineas prize at Mallory Park and at Brands Hatch he swept the board by winning the 350 c.c. and 500 c.c. and Race of the South events. These end-of-season races in England enabled the glamour boy to capture the hearts as well as the admiration of the British public and he was acclaimed Man of the Year in the annual poll organized by the national magazine *Motor Cycle News*.

Agostini has great box-office appeal and big crowds turn out whenever he's around. He is young, incredibly handsome and has a carefree personality and wealthy background which makes him a piece of pure magic in the eyes of his thousands of fans throughout the world. It has never been necessary for him to work for a living. On leaving school he drifted into his father's flourishing transport and road-building business without much dedication. His heart was never in it.

Ago admits: 'If I wanted a day off I took it, and as I got more and more interested in racing, so I took more and more time off until I stopped working for him completely.' His parents were rich enough to keep him free from financial worries but they viewed with concern his developing interest, as a young man, in motor cycle sport. They tried to discourage him, but he was adamant. He'd been fascinated by bikes from early on.

At the age of nine he rode a Vespa scooter, at 10 he owned a Bianchi moped and when 15 he had two machines, a Parilla on which he competed in local trials, and a 175 c.c. Moto-Guzzi roadster.

His first serious, though modest, outings were hillclimbs and Italian domestic road races (on a private 175 c.c. Morini). The Italian factory then lent him a works machine and he entered his first major road race in 1963. Riding a 175 c.c. Morini he led for the first lap; then machine trouble put him out. But Morini had seen enough of Agostini's courage and style and were convinced that here was a home-bred rider of outstanding talent. The following year he became their number one runner and beat Tarquino Provini to win the 250 c.c. Italian championship. In 1965 he signed for MV and the Agostini legend began.

From then on it was world competition in a big way, with Agostini's greatest successes coming against his old team-mate Mike Hailwood, struggling now with machine problems on his giant Honda. Now it was Agostini, racing the Italian marque to world victories. After his sensational triumph in winning the 500 c.c. world championship in 1966, he beat Mike to the title again in 1967 and set about making it three in a row. Agostini's contract with MV was due to expire at the end of 1968. What then? 'Next year I will do both car and motor cycle racing. Ferrari want me to drive one of their Formula I cars, but I shall continue with bikes,' he said.

So it seems that during 1969 at least, Giacomo Agostini will be around the circuits, a prospect to delight everyone in the game—except, of course, those who ride against him.

115

HUGH ANDERSON

116

117

118

The world championships have seldom had a serious challenger from New Zealand. The obvious and outstanding exception is Auckland's Hugh Anderson, who reputedly rode an ancient Douglas round the family farm when only ten years old.

He turned to road racing via scrambling and arrived in Europe in 1960. He rode for AJS and Norton and then joined Suzuki in 1961. He had successfully contested a number of New Zealand championships and quick success might have been expected of him. This was the time of Suzuki's early development, however, and their machines were hardly competitive. But the blend of the Japanese factory's technical skill, resulting in faster machinery, and the New Zealander's riding ability was to bring international success. In 1963 Hugh Anderson completed the season as a double world champion—taking the 50 c.c. and 125 c.c. titles. He took the 'tiddler' crown once more the following year. In 1965 Ralph Bryans, from Ireland, dominated the 50 c.c. class, but Hugh took premier honours once again in the 125 c.c. category.

Anderson's early non-works successes were achieved on 350 and 500 c.c. machines, principally AJS, Norton and Matchless, and he switched to the lighter classes without difficulty. He maintained that the two-strokes were much more difficult to ride. His assessment: 'You've got to concentrate all the time because the bikes are light and tend to leap about. The tyres are narrow and the tyre pressure high—altogether the two-strokes are much more lively.' After his successes of 1963, '64 and '65, Hugh Anderson's name was absent from the world championship chart. Machine problems had a good deal to do with this and Suzuki had to work hard on their mounts in an attempt to give them a better spread of power. Anderson's World Championship in the 125 c.c. class in 1965 was gained over twelve events. At the Nürburgring, in the West German Grand Prix, he established a new record lap and a new race record speed. He was first in this race, first again in the Spanish, and also in the French Grand Prix, where his 2 minute 34.9 second lap was a record at 94.41 m.p.h. He was unplaced in the Isle of Man, though he established the lap record, raising it by almost 2 m.p.h.

At the Dutch TT he gained third place, behind Mike Duff on a Yamaha and Yoshimi Katayama (Suzuki). After being unplaced in East Germany, Czechoslovakia and Ireland, he finished the year in brilliant style, winning the three final Grands Prix in Italy, Finland and Japan. Appropriately the season's final triumph was on the 3.7-mile Suzuka circuit. Suzuki gained the manufacturers' world championship that year in the 125 c.c. class.

JIM REDMAN

It takes an abundance of talent, plenty of courage, fine machinery and a reasonable quota of good fortune to become a world champion just once. When you beat the rest of the world *six times*, it is obvious that you are a man of extraordinary ability. Such a man is Jim Redman, quiet, unspectacular, sanguine—but also superbly stylish in the saddle and a master at his craft.

Redman was born in Britain, but went to Rhodesia in 1952 and gained all his outstanding honours for that country. With vague thoughts already niggling at the back of his mind that motor cycle racing would be an exciting sport to try, he met John Love, who was then moving from motor bikes to car racing. The two men became firm friends and Redman helped Love to prepare his Formula 3 Cooper-Norton. Redman made no secret of his enthusiasm for motor cycles and in return for the help he had so willingly given, John Love let him borrow his grand prix Triumph and all his racing clothing for a meeting. Redman finished seventh and was on his way. He was further encouraged by Beppe Castellani and Ken Robas, big names on the African Continent. Redman's progress was swift. He was soon a major force in Rhodesia. Castellani pipped him to the 500 c.c. Rhodesian championship, but Redman collected the 350 c.c. title. Now he set his sights on the major European events, the ambition of most motor cycle racers. His first race was at Brands Hatch, where he finished in the first three. This was recognized as a fine performance against established riders such as Bob McIntyre, Alastair King and an embryo sensation by the name of Mike Hailwood. It was also an occasion for learning. Jim had to adapt his 'flat-out' Rhodesian racing technique to the tight-cornered, short circuits of Britain.

In 1959 Jim Redman, having been unable to more than glimpse at the European scene, returned to Rhodesia and retired from motor cycling. The urge remained, however, and he decided to return to Europe for just one more season of racing during 1960. His ambition was a works contract and he hoped to impress the East German MZ team manager, Walter Kaaden, sufficiently to be offered rides in the 250 and 125 c.c. classes. MZ, however, were now to secure his services.

There's an old saying that suggests there is no coming back after retirement. Redman made a mockery of it. Through an accident to Tom Phillis, he got an opportunity with Honda, who were then trying to muscle in on the motor cycling world scene. He recognized his big chance and made no mistake. He made his Honda debut at the Dutch TT in Assen, having been brought in at short notice. Without experience on the Japanese machines he finished seventh in the

250 c.c. event and fourth in the 125 c.c. He showed plenty of promise and when Honda mounted a major assault on world racing the following year, Redman was invited to join their team.

Success came quickly and sensationally. In 1962 he was both 350 c.c. and 250 c.c. world champion, repeated his double triumph the following year and, after being eclipsed by the ultra-fast Yamaha lightweights of Phil Read, went on to win the 350 c.c. World title again in 1964 and yet again in 1965. The astonishing record read: six world championships in four years. He was awarded the MBE. For all his world records and high-speed performances in the region of 130-140 m.p.h., Jim Redman, now retired from the European scene, had a cautious approach to racing. He never went faster than was necessary to beat the opposition, and the slenderest of margins was good enough. Not for Redman, speed for speed's sake. The object was to win the race. That's all. For this reason he lacked the glamour and swashbuckling character of some of his contemporaries, although his intelligent racing was never in doubt.

119

120

121

122

121 The late Bob McIntyre at the Isle of Man.
122 Mac makes ground at 99.58 m.p.h. on the 250 c.c. Honda.

BOB McINTYRE

Bob McIntyre was one of the sport's really great riders, an exciting record-breaker and, not least, an immense credit to the sport and his home town of Glasgow. Many observers believe him to have been the finest rider never to win a world championship. He had a string of outstanding rides, both as a privateer and a works teamster, and seemed all set to become a world champion when a crash put him out of the running. There was to be no second chance. Gilera, for whom Bob had been racing, retired from the sport, and, back again on private mounts, his machinery was never quick enough to challenge the dominant MVs. For about a decade, motor cycle sport was 'Bob Mac's' life. In the years leading up to 1962 he was one of the very big names in racing. Then came the fateful day at Oulton Park in August 1962 when the great Scottish rider crashed and died as a result of his injuries. At 33 years of age and at the peak of his career, Bob's racing days had tragically ended. He left behind a wealth of memories including the first 100 m.p.h. lap of the Isle of Man Mountain Circuit and a Junior/Senior TT double. Then there was that almost unbelievable 141 m.p.h. at Monza in 1957 on a 350 c.c. four-cylinder Gilera when he shattered the world one-hour record.

Bob's motor-cycle baptism was on a 500 c.c. 16H Norton, 1931 model, which cost him just £12. It all started from that point. In the competitive sense it was scrambling which first captivated Bob. After seeing a couple of meetings he began entering and won a number of club events. Then he saw his first road race in a public park at Kirkcaldy and reckoned he might do as well as some of those taking part. Bob McIntyre, the road racer, was on his way. He entered his first amateur event on a borrowed 350 c.c. BSA Gold Star, competed in four events, won three and fell off in the other. His £15 winnings fired his ambition and he soon began to make real progress. In 1952 he took second place in the Senior Manx Grand Prix on a Junior machine and second place in the Junior TT. In the 1961 and 1962 Lightweight 250 c.c. TTs he lapped at over 99 m.p.h. on Honda machines. In 1954 Bob was a works rider for AJS and afterwards joined with Joe Potts, the Scottish tuner who became his sponsor, riding Nortons and AJSs. He took Joe's Nortons into second place in the Junior TT and fifth place in the Senior TT of 1955 and collected many short-circuit firsts.

At that time Geoff Duke, world champion, was also team leader of Gilera and he was impressed with Bob's achievements. At the end of the season Gilera offered the talented Scot a works contract, but by that time Bob had already made his plans to ride Joe Potts' machinery again for the following season.

73

FRITZ SCHEIDEGGER

Gilera were not easily put off. They repeated their offer a year later and Bob signed to ride the Italian bikes in classic races. Said Bob later: 'I had discussed the question with Joe Potts. He knew that to win classic races I needed better mounts than he could provide for me.' It was just not possible to match the multi-cylinder Italian flyers, the Gileras and MVs, on a private, single-cylinder British machine. It was as Gilera's rider in 1957 that he gained immortal fame by his sensational TT double and that first ever 100 m.p.h. lap.

McIntyre was tremendously impressed with the Gilera organization. On a brief visit to the firm's Italian headquarters he was thrilled by Signor Gilera's attitude, the enthusiasm and excellence of the mechanics and by the highly professional approach. Then, when he seemed set for the highest honours, Gilera retired.

And almost as a postscript to his career with the Italian factory, came that record-breaking last fling at Monza. What a postscript! The world's one-hour standing start record stood to the credit of Ray Amm at 133 m.p.h. on a 500 c.c. Norton. Bob was to ride his 350 c.c. machine, a four-cylinder model of the type he had raced in Junior events. Only once before had he been to Monza, but he was to shatter the record by 8 m.p.h. Bob described the experience: 'I was soon hitting the banking at 155 m.p.h. Because of the bumps I had to stand up on the footrests, holding on to the handlebars grimly as though I was riding in a scramble. Then, after 15 minutes, the bike stopped; it was a magneto fault.'

McIntyre was ready to call it a day, but the Gilera chiefs persuaded him to stay. They fitted a new magneto and Mac was off again. In his own book McIntyre described the historic occasion: 'fifteen minutes of flat-out racing had been wasted. Up through the gears I went again. Round and round I tore, the throttle wide open, just concentrating on staying on. My legs ached, my arms throbbed from the constant vibration. At the end of the hour they put out the flag for me and I came in. They had very nearly to lift me from the machine. My wrists were swelling up and my feet were sore. The instep of one of my boots had been broken by the jarring of the footrest beneath it.'

This was perhaps Bob McIntyre's greatest hour. When his record was finally bettered by Mike Hailwood (on a 500 c.c. MV) seven years later, it was Mike himself who paid a well-deserved tribute to Bob's achievement: 'There never was a more magnificent ride than that made by Bob on the Monza track in 1957. Only riders who have attempted that circuit can truly appreciate the sheer guts and brilliant riding which made Bob's effort possible.'

For eleven consecutive years, BMW won the 500 c.c. world sidecar championship. For eleven consecutive years their outstanding machines, with their great power and shattering reliability, were ridden by West German aces. Then in 1965 along came gentlemanly, bespectacled Fritz Scheidegger of Switzerland. He took over from the West German riders at their speciality event, but the tradition was in part continued, for Fritz won the championship on a BMW-powered outfit.

The tall Swiss champion had already established a firm reputation in his home country and as early as 1957 was Swiss 350 c.c., 500 c.c. solo and sidecar champion for both road-racing and grass tracks. An Englishman, John Robinson, shared his 'world' triumph in 1965 and no success was more hard fought, for Scheidegger and Robinson had been runners-up on three previous occasions. Indeed, that world title looked to be forever elusive and Fritz almost retired with the ambition unfulfilled in 1964, but the burning desire to gain the crown kept him racing. He returned to the tracks at the start of 1966 and it was at the TTs of that year that he innocently became involved in a major sensation. He and Robinson won the Sidecar TT by less than a second from Germany's Max Deubel, but then... uproar! There was a protest that Scheidegger had infringed the fuel regulations by not using the petrol supplied at the meeting. Fritz maintained that he had declared his choice of fuel at the scrutineering and there had been no objection then. An official confirmed his statement, but he was disqualified.

There was an outcry, however, and he was reinstated as winner. He continued racing that year and was world champion again. During the close season and in spite of ill-health, Fritz and John Robinson decided to contest a full round of classic events during the forthcoming year in an attempt to gain the world championship for three consecutive seasons. It was no secret that, this ambition fulfilled, Scheidegger would retire.

But tragedy loomed and without warning struck early in the season at a domestic meeting at Mallory Park. He had started the race badly, but was beginning to thrill the crowds with a fine demonstration of technique. He and Robinson were moving up the field in a strong challenge and had set up the fastest lap. Then came disaster. As he went into the hairpin, the outfit hit the barrier. Fritz Scheidegger was killed. John Robinson was injured, but recovered. After the crash, he announced his retirement. Few champions, if any, enjoyed more respect than Fritz Scheidegger, and his fatal accident, its personal tragedy aside, was a great loss to a sport which held him in the highest regard as a racer, sportsman and gentleman.

123 Scheidegger (left) and Robinson at Solitude, 1964.
124 Fritz and John at Clermont Ferrand.
125 Gary Nixon and the amazing trophy that goes with winning the Daytona 200.

GARY NIXON

123 Scheidegger (left) and Robinson at Solitude, 1964.
124 Fritz and John at Clermont Ferrand.
125 Gary Nixon and the amazing trophy that goes with winning the Daytona 200.

Success in American motor-cycle racing calls for exceptional all-round ability and to do well you must be an expert on both road and dirt tracks similar to short-circuit racing and long-track speedway. One of the unquestionable experts, with a remarkable all-round talent, is a scintillating character called Gary Nixon, an Oklahoma-born racer with close-cropped hair and a single-minded approach to the racing business which brings him a steady succession of victories. Gary became the Grand National Champion for 1967 after a season of tremendous riding and 'cliff-hanger' situations which kept the fans yelling for more right up to the end. The Oklahoma City race at the end of the season was the decider. George Roeder, the Harley-Davidson rider, was capable of taking the title, but he had to win the 'Oklahoma City' and Nixon had to finish no better than sixth position. Roeder had a good chance. Gary would be riding with a fractured bone in his hand. Adding spice to the situation was Roeder's undisputed ability on the half-mile ovals and Nixon's failure to qualify in the previous points race on a half-mile oval only a month before.

But Gary produced an overdose of that Nixon determination. He finished second, while Roeder could do no better than fourth after being the fastest qualifier. This completed a season of sensational racing from which firebrand Nixon was reputed to have made $40,000.

Now he would like to specialise in road racing, which he prefers and where he is most successful, but with the 'all round' character of American racing, it is impossible without moving outside the country. What *is* possible is that Gary will be seen on some of the grand prix circuits of Europe. He came near to such competition in 1966 when he was set to ride one of the four-cylinder Yamahas in the Japanese Grand Prix, but a damaged hand robbed him of the chance. Money is another problem. Grand prix riding could well reduce his earnings, not a palatable thought.

Nixon excels at road racing. For Yamaha he won the 100-mile lightweight race at Daytona in 1967 and on the following day secured the 200-mile for Triumph against keen and concentrated Harley-Davidson competition. On the dirt, where combat is close and fierce his style is equally exciting. Riding the smoother one-milers, he slings his machine into 100 m.p.h. breathtaking broadsides. There is plenty of showmanship in the Nixon character and his normally cool demeanour can suddenly hot-up with outbursts which temporarily lose him friends and strain relationships with colleagues. But once astride his mount, clad in his white, stripey leathers, Gary Nixon shows them all who's in charge. During 1967 he scored a total of 508 points in the nat-

126 Gary on his way to victory in the '67 Daytona 100.
Three world-beaters: 127 Hailwood pushing his 496 c.c. Kirby
Matchless round the curves at Brands.

128 Agostini—500 c.c. World Champion.
129 Scheidegger leads the field for the last time. Shortly
afterwards he crashed and was killed. Mallory Park, 26 March, 1967.

ional-championship table while George Roeder, at number two, was 57 points behind. In other events Gary piled up the points. He won the 200 miler at Daytona, as already mentioned, the 100 mile Laconia and the 75 mile race at Carlsbad in California, giving him victory in three out of four events. He also won at Portland, Oregon, and was first again in the 25-lap short-track event at Santa Fé.

Although Gary was well fancied for the title, the season brought its crises for the flamboyant young American. The Harley-Davidson teamsters had a glimpse of success when Nixon lost the lead in August by a close margin to Mert Lawwill, but Gary recovered the lead with his victory on a Triumph Tiger Cub in the short-track Santa Fé event. Nixon panicked his fans again when he lost ground at San José in September and then at Ascot Park. A flat rear tyre, after he had moved up to fourth place, slid him further into decline at Sacramento, where Roeder won to move into the lead with only two meetings left. But at Carlsbad, in the 75-mile race, Gary made no mistake and then went on to the final, deciding event at Oklahoma City.

Gary's wife Mary, who comes from England, and his father and mother, follow his career closely. At the start of 1968 the flame-haired rider showed he had lost none of the old Nixon technique. At Houston's fabulous Astrodome in Texas, before 32,000 fans, he won the Expert event on a Triumph, ahead of the Harley-Davidson riders Mert Lawwill and Cal Rayborn, and was on his way again. For him the future seems bright.

127

126

128

129

CONTINENTAL CIRCUS

Motor cycle sport was at first essentially parochial. You
took yourself and your bike to the nearest track and
that was that. Very quickly, the better riders searched
further for competition. First in their own country,
later outside it. In such circumstances was born the
Continental Circus. Manufacturers interested in seeing
the sport grow thrust it ahead by giving financial support, providing machines and mechanics, signing con-
tracts with riders, providing fuel, start and prize money.
A society developing in sophistication, and a world
shrinking through speedy and frequent air-travel, facilitated its coming-of-age. Today a works contract is
the ambition of most career-bent riders. It means a
lucrative salary, fringe benefits and membership of the
circus—competing in one race after another on the
grand prix circuits of the world.

There was no formal inauguration of the continental
circus. It simply grew into being. The foreign riders
entered in the French Grand Prix of 1914 contributed
to its formation. The fact that war came and the race
never took place is irrelevant. By 1920 the French
Grand Prix was again established, though it attracted
little interest in Britain, whose riders had seen quite
enough of France to want to return so soon, even
under different circumstances. But this was a temporary
attitude. The French Grand Prix was augmented in
1921 by similar races in Belgium and Italy. The German
Grand Prix was added in 1923 and then came the
Hungarian, Dutch, Austrian and Swedish Grands Prix.
The continental circus was well on its way, though
still very much in embryo. There was no question of
the same cluster of riders competing in all the events
as now. British entries, for instance, were confined fo

130 Jesse Baker on a Scott during the 1920 Paris-Nice Rally.
131 Clarry Wood (45) and Leslie Guy (46), Scott riders in the Paris-Nice Rally—at the Nice end.

132 Alexander speeding his Douglas through the pine forest on the French Grand Prix course at Le Mans in 1920.

a number of years to the French and Belgian Grands Prix, but by 1925 the more adventurous riders were probing farther afield. Frank Longman tackled the German that year on an AJS and made the fastest 350 c.c. lap: and Jock Porter on a New Gerrard won the lightweight class at the Italian Grand Prix.

1926 provides an interesting comparison with today, when British riders are supreme on foreign machines. British machines won all classes of the Dutch TT that year—but astonishingly, all the riders were from Holland! In 1927 Britain competed in five major continental events and in six the following year. The organization behind such outings was improving and being mounted by this time in a much more business-like way.

One of the outstanding exponents of the 'circus' between the wars, and perhaps the most successful of all, was Jimmy Guthrie. In 1935 and 1936 he won the 500 c.c. class of nine European Grand Prix races in succession. The following year, he won the 350 and 500 c.c. classes of the Swiss Grand Prix and the 500 c.c. of the Belgian. Then came the German Grand Prix in which this great Norton team member lost his life.

Immediately before the second world war, and again immediately after it, Freddie Frith was a regular member of the 'circus' and in 1949 he won the 350 c.c. events at all the major continental meetings. With the passing of years some circuits were to lose their grand prix status while others gained it, but in Holland the circuit at Assen was popular right at the start and gained further affection as time went on. In the early days the Dutch TT course was about the width of an English country lane and had dykes on either side; it was very flat. The Dutch TT was to become known for its gaiety and carnival atmosphere and, of course, for the vast crowds who flock into Northern Holland to see the racing on the 4.8-mile circuit. Its fine left—and right—handers, some of them banked, call for great riding skill, and extend the capabilities of even the best riders.

The 1950 Dutch TT marked the twenty-fifth anniversary of this event and, as always, the organization was efficient and the atmosphere enthusiastic. There were enormous crowds. This was to become renowned as the year in which tyre troubles completely wrecked the British challenge. In the 125 c.c. class Italy took

131

132

133

the first five places, their home riders mounted on Mondial (1st, 2nd, 3rd, and 4th) and MV machinery (5th). British Nortons and Velocettes dominated the 350 c.c. event, but it was Italy once more in the Senior race. Thirty-eight machines started, including three Gileras, two MVs and a Guzzi from Italy. There was a massive contingent from Britain of twenty Nortons, five Triumphs, three AJSs, two Velocettes and a Triumph-powered AJS. A BMW was being ridden by a Dutchman, Piet Knijnenburg.

As the machines raced away at the start, it was first blood to the Italians, with Artesiani on an MV in the lead, though Les Graham made a successful challenge and took the lead for a short time. Italy had consolidated her position at the end of the first lap and Bandirola and Pagani, who had won the previous year's Dutch TT, had moved to the front. Then came the British trio of Les Graham, Duke and Lockett. Masetti's Gilera was there too, in sixth position. During the second lap Masetti made a wonderful effort and took the lead, but by the third lap he had slumped to third place. Pagani was now at the front, with Geoff Duke for

Britain challenging strongly. With fourteen laps still to go there was every possibility of this being a really eventful race. Already there had been plenty of exciting racing, with rapidly-changing positions at the front. For the fourth and fifth laps Gileras held first, second and third places, though Duke and Graham were pressing strongly. Then on the sixth lap the interest and spirit of the race evaporated. Tyre trouble was responsible for the retirement of almost all members of the British AJS and Norton works teams. For a time Dickie Dale kept the Union Jack flying but then he too was brought in.

Gileras were able to sweep clear, but Harry Hinton on a privately-entered Norton rode the race of his life. On the thirteenth lap he even managed to press ahead of Bandirola, to take second place, and the Italian certainly hadn't been wasting time—at 95.55 m.p.h. he had made the fastest lap of the day. There was a momentary surge of renewed interest as Masetti, riding in the lead, came in to refuel at the same time as Hinton. But the challenge was too much for Hinton and he finished the race in third position, Masetti won the race,

81

135 The winners of the first Dutch TT, 1925. Left to right: H. Bieze (New Imperial 350 c.c.), A. Wuring (BSA 250 c.c.) and P. van Wijngaarden (Norton 500 c.c.).

136 An early pile-up. Charlie Hough on an AJS comes to grief, while Angelo Martinelli opens up the throttle of his Motosacoche and makes good his escape; Dutch TT 1928.

135 The winners of the first Dutch TT, 1925. Left to right: H. Bieze (New Imperial 350 c.c.), A. Wuring (BSA 250 c.c.) and P. van Wijngaarden (Norton 500 c.c.).

136 An early pile-up. Charlie Hough on an AJS comes to grief, while Angelo Martinelli opens up the throttle of his Motosacoche and makes good his escape; Dutch TT 1928.

Pagani was in second place and Bandirola came fourth.

If nothing else, this Dutch TT proved again what an essential part is played in the racing game by the accessory manufacturers. Weaknesses are quickly exposed. Certainly a racing machine, however advanced mechanically, is no better than its tyres.

In 1949 the Grand Prix had been given a face lift. Before that year the Grand Prix d'Europe was allocated to a single grand prix meeting at which the winners in each class became European champions. A rider could therefore win all his other Grand Prix races, but if, for instance, mechanical failure in this one vital meeting put him down the field, he did not qualify for European Championship honours. When the Fédération Internationale Motocycliste reconstituted the grand prix they made it much fairer, more sensible, and acknowledged the importance of a consistently good performance. The new competition called for greater knowledge and skill on the part of the rider. It now became essential for him to race well at a number of meetings. That meant he was required to ride fast and skilfully over a longer period, his machines had to be more reliable, and it was essential for him to have a working knowledge and understanding of all the grand prix circuits. But the honours were so much greater, for the best overall rider became not the European champion, but world champion.

Before each season a series of meetings are nominated as World Classic events. Points on a sliding scale from eight to one are awarded to the riders occupying the first six places. Eight points go to the winner, six for second place, four for third, three for fourth, two for fifth and one for sixth. To win a championship it is not necessary for a rider to contest every event. He must,

however, race in more than half the championship events in any particular class: if there are ten 350 c.c. championship races in a year, the most points obtained in half this total number plus one (i.e. six races) count in deciding the results of the championship. The system and its method of deciding ties is not without its complications, and as recently as 1967 there was total confusion at the end of the season in the 250 c.c. class, for Mike Hailwood and Phil Read ended the year with the same number of points. In some quarters Phil Read was hailed the victor while others were equally convinced that Hailwood was champion. Mike finally got the decision. His fifty points, including five wins, to Phil's fifty points, including four wins, was sufficient under a Fédération Internationale Motocycliste rule, revised in 1964, to give him the title.

Back in 1949 the newly constituted grand prix programme was recognized as a more realistic championship and gave further impetus to the continental circus. In that first year under the new rules, Italy and Britain shared the top honours. An AJS ridden by Les Graham secured the 500 c.c. world championship, Freddie Frith was 350 c.c. champion riding a Velocette, while Bruno Ruffo on a Guzzi and Nello Pagani on a Mondial were champions in the 250 and 125 c.c. categories (a complete list of world champions from 1949 to the present time is included at the end of this book).

As time went on, the championships became completely dominated by factory-sponsored works teams. The privateer, always sadly at a disadvantage, was virtually priced out of the world market. The high cost involved in entering the classics, all in different countries, was prohibitive for most of the private riders— even with the help of sponsors. For the private entrant

137 A 600 c.c. DKW 'UL' ridden by factory rider Hans Schuhmann in the 1937 Swiss Grand Prix at Berne. Cornering with both hands on one side of the handlebars was a German speciality.

138 Harry Daniell waving in his team-mates in the Dutch TT of 1950, the 'year of the bad tyres.'

139 The start of a pre-war 500 c.c. race at the Nürburgring.

140 The start of the 1926 Dutch TT. The starting area was then extremely narrow by modern standards—only four metres, in fact.

141 The winners of the 1933 Dutch TT: Ivan Goor (Belgium, 175 c.c. Benelli); G. de Ridder (first Dutchman, Grindlay Peerless-Rudge 250 c.c.); Ted Mellors (Britain, 250 c.c. New Imperial); Piet van Wijngaarden (Holland, 350 c.c. Norton); Stanley Woods (Ireland, 350 c.c. Norton).

142 Joe Craig, Norton's manager before the war, consulting his top riders, Harry Daniell and Freddie Frith.

143 A Nazi salute for Jimmy Guthrie, winner of the 1935 500 c.c. German Grand Prix; on the left is Joe Craig, on the right Herr Hühnlein, German Minister for Sport.

144 Admirers of the AJS 'Porcupine': A. J. Bell (in leathers), Les Graham (on the bike), 'Cabby' Cooper (with camera), Jock West of the AMC (with sunglasses) and on the right in leathers· Reg Armstrong.

the off-track worries were infinitely more keenly felt. While the factory rider was able to concentrate on the full-time job of racing, the individual entrant had to be much more actively involved with preparing his machine, getting from one place to another: and hanging over the whole operation, the spectre of the possibility of a crash.

As a career, the world classic meetings now hold little interest for the non-works rider. His net income can be far greater from consistent success and lesser, non-classic, Continental circuits. But competition in some of the classic events is still essential for a young rider to attract the serious interest and attention of a major factory, and of course the prestige of a grand prix victory is always extremely tempting to any rider.

Road racing thus divided itself into two operations— the home-based riders indigenous to their countries, who race on local tracks; and the works boys paid for and supported by the major factories. Of the former group Derek Minter has been one of the most successful. At Brands Hatch in England, he followed the example of John Surtees and was King of the Kent circuit for many years. A superbly stylish rider with a shrewd ability to 'read' and interpret a race, there is no doubt that Minter had the ability to become one of the greatest factory riders, but his persistent individuality made it difficult for him to settle as a member of a team. For this reason Derek Minter is the classic example

of a brilliant rider to whom the highest prestige of out-and-out World Championship racing has been denied.

Classic events have this prestige because the manu-facturers pump most of their money into this sphere of racing. The cost of maintaining a team of riders in the field nowadays is astronomical. The top riders command high salaries (e.g. Hailwood's estimated con-tract with Honda—around £30,000 a year), and in addition there is the building and upkeep of the ma-chines, the support of a team of mechanics, extensive transportation and travelling charges and the usual costs of accommodation.

Being a world champion has a giant-size ring about it and the experts of the day, as long ago as 1905, were competing in the World's Motor Cycle Championship, billed as the first recognised 'world' event ever to be held. Seventeen crack riders entered, though only ten took part in the racing at the fast, banked circuit at Zurenbourg Velodrome in Antwerp.

Conditions stipulated that machines weigh under 50 kilogrammes (110 lbs) with the usual three kilogramme allowance for accumulators; distance, 5 kilometres, to be ridden in heats; and a final, flying start. Reported *Motor Cycle* of 10 July 1905: 'Olieslaegers, the Belgian crack, should have a good chance of scoring, for he knows every inch of the track, and has not yet been defeated, riding at a sixty miles an hour gait with all the comfort and confidence of a real champion. How-

145 Imatra Circuit, Finland: the start of the 1967 250 c.c. Grand Prix.
146 Repair work and relaxation for the Honda team at Brno in Czechoslovakia (1967).
147 The start of a 50 c.c. race at Hockenheim in 1967.

145

146

ever, Franz Hoffmann the dare-devil German, Joseph Giuppone the Italian, Cissac, Fossier, and half a dozen other experts will, no doubt, have something to say in the matter, and let us hope to see Barnes, Chase, or Martin, etc., among the starters.'

The four who qualified for the final were Jan Olieslaegers (Belgium), Alexander Anzani (Italy), André Pernelle (France) and Louis Bac (France). The Belgian ace, practically invincible on the circuit's high, bumpy bankings, looked set to secure the title. His technique was shrewder than that of his opponents and he took a lower line on the banking, thereby gaining time. He was fully fifty yards ahead of Anzani, his nearest challenger, and was comfortably maintaining the pace, but a burst tyre a few laps from the end brought him down on one of the straights; although he somersaulted a number of times, he was unhurt. Anzani went on to win the 1,000 franc prize money and Italy gained the first 'world' crown.

148 The start of the 350 c.c. race in the 1959 Dutch TT. This race was dominated from start to finish by a duel between Hocking (24) and Brown (2), Brown winning by the narrowest of margins.

149

150

149 Assen in 1950—the Dutch Grand Prix.
150 Spa—the 1950 Belgian Grand Prix.
151 H. L. Cooper riding through Peel in the 1908 Isle of Man Tourist Trophy.

FAMOUS RACING CIRCUITS

Early racing was an uninhibited affair in which both riders and machines displayed more courage, spirit and dash than science. There was a spontaneity about these pioneering efforts which demanded nothing more than a ribbon of road or track, a machine to ride and someone else to beat. As the approach to racing became more sophisticated and scientific, having the best possible conditions became increasingly important. Professionalism, prestige, progress, finance—all played their part in the development, not only of the machine and the riders' approach to racing, but of the character of the sport itself. Roads which had involuntarily become racing routes began to establish a reputation as race circuits and assumed a new identity. There were exceptions: Brooklands for instance, was constructed specifically for racing, and others, later on, were to be built to accommodate the growing interest in racing both bikes and cars. These combined with more natural courses, and nowadays the best and most demanding remain to test the skill of the world's top riders and the speed and dependability of highly expensive machines.

The Isle of Man 37¾-mile Mountain Circuit continues to be generally acknowledged as the most arduous, demanding and yet the most natural course in the world. The road wanders through villages and towns, sweeps through open country, twists and winds unexpectedly through beautiful countryside, doubles back on itself and, of course, goes up, over and down Mount Snaefell. The TT races are the world's most punishing test for riders and machines, and only the best survive. For the many thousands who have a special interest in motor-cycle racing, the Isle of Man during TT week is a paradise. For two weeks every year the entire island lives, breathes and sleeps motor cycles, and the countryside around the course provides natural vantage points on which the fans cluster.

Another of the early-established courses is in Holland, where the Assen circuit, now cut to some 4¾ miles of private and public roads, has been the home of the Dutch TT since the early days of motor cycle racing, although the present course, incorporating part of the

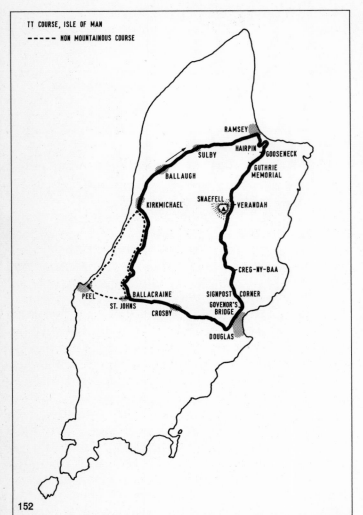

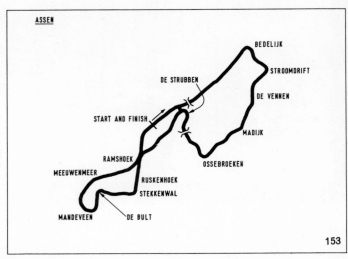

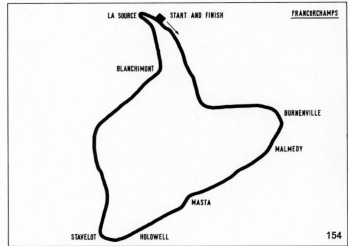

old, was first used after World War II. There is a carnival atmosphere at this event with fairs and parades to supplement the racing. The course now has plenty of twists and bends to keep riders alert—and average speeds down. But success in Holland requires a measure of skilful riding not needed on the more open, rolling circuits. As recorded earlier in this book, the Assen course was originally about the width of an English country lane and had a deep dyke on each side. It was not altogether surprising that plenty of riders had their 'moments' at Assen. Ted Mellors used to tell the story of a practice lap he did on the pillion with Matt Wright (who prepared machines) riding up front. Matt apparently attempted to take a corner too fast (quite 10 m.p.h. reported Ted) and although neither rider parted company from the machine, it was a near thing.

In 'The Racing Game' by G.S. Davison, Freddie Frith tells of the amusing occasion when he sped round a corner at Assen to be confronted by a cow: 'We rushed around pretty smartly, myself a few feet in front of Ken (team mate Kenneth Bills), and you can imagine the sort of shock we had when we saw a cow dashing wildly about in the middle of the road, chased by an excited Dutch policeman. There was nothing much Ken and I could do about it, for it was impossible to attempt to brake—all we could do was to put our heads down and hope for the best'.

Far less demanding than Assen, in terms of riding skill, is the noted circuit in Belgium, at Francorchamps, near Spa. Here it is the machines which are in open competition and, other than the hairpin at La Source just before the pits, there is little to worry the rider on this 9-mile long circuit where the fastest machines generally take the honours. The West German Grand Prix has 'moved house' a number of times. The early Hockenheim circuit again provided little scope for the skills of the rider and the two straights enabled lap speeds in the region of 130 m.p.h. as early as the mid-1950s. Few riders were sorry when the construction of

155 Monza: the start of the 250 c.c. class in the 1959 Grand Prix des Nations.
156 Monza.

157 The Nürburgring in 1965.
158 The Nürburgring.

155

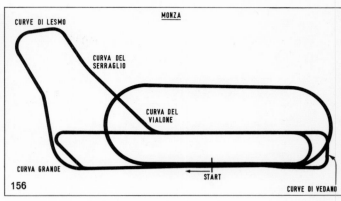

156

157

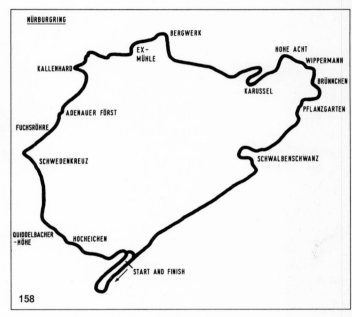

158

an autobahn meant the redesigning of the circuit, or when the meeting was staged on the Solitude circuit, set in picturesque country. Occasionally too, the grand prix was held at the Nürburgring, possibly the most complicated course in Europe. It extends for more than 14 miles and includes 170 bends and corners, not to mention gradients, bridges, camber and surface changes, to keep the rider thinking all the time. The short 4.8-mile circuit chosen for the 1965 and 1968 grands prix, for instance, was most exacting, and in the 500 c.c. class speeds were in the mid-eighties, against the near-120 m.p.h. registered on average by the top three on the Belgian circuit. With machines usually so near to one another in performance, races nowadays are very often won or lost by the skill of the rider at the bends.

Monza in Italy has established a world-wide reputation for its race meetings. Its 3½-mile motor-cycle circuit is pleasantly situated in a park and although there are a number of sweeping curves, there are only

a couple of definite corners. It is regarded very much as a 'burn-up' by those taking part and if you've got a fast machine you may well be in among the leaders at the end. Caldarella reached 121.73 m.p.h. in 1964!

The French Grand Prix circuit at Clermont Ferrand was seen to be in complete contrast to the lap at Monza, when it was first used in 1959: the longest straight was only 650 yards and a variety of really tight corners quickly demonstrated—or exposed—a rider's skill! The French Grand Prix was one of the very earliest Continental races to capture the attention of British adventurers. As early as 1914 it was described as 'the most important event of its kind on the Continent' and about one third of the entries for this race were from Britain. But the first world war intervened and it never took place. During its early history the French Grand Prix was run on a different circuit every year—at the famous Le Mans for instance, in 1921, Strasbourg the following year, and over a circuit near Tours in 1923.

The circuit at Dundrod where the Ulster Grand Prix

159

161

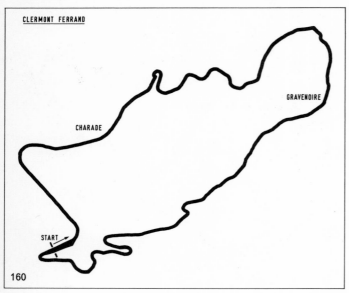

160

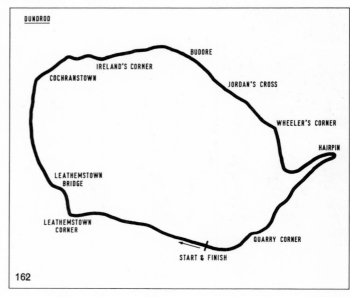

162

is staged is $7\frac{1}{2}$ miles round, and came into use in 1953. Some riders love it; others hate it. Bob McIntyre, for instance, said it was his favourite. Derek Minter, on the other hand, despised it and criticised it strongly for the state of its roads, which he thought in worse condition than some of the most neglected rural roads in England. He also had uncomplimentary things to say about the off-track organization and the facilities given to competitors, but he thought the configuration of the course itself good. There are plenty of bends and hills and one particularly acute right-hand hairpin.

The grand prix circuit in East Germany is at Sachsenring and is almost $5\frac{1}{2}$ miles round. Competing there is a great experience, according to Jim Redman, and certainly crowds are among the largest in the world, with more than 200,000 witnessing the racing at times. Jim considered them to be probably the most ardent race fans anywhere, many of them travelling and sometimes hitch-hiking from as far away as East Berlin, 140 miles distant. There are many other notable road-race circuits including those in Spain, at Barcelona,

Czechoslovakia, Sweden and Finland. The most famous American circuit is at Daytona, Florida, which is a little over 3 miles round.

Of the newer circuits special note must be made of that at Suzuka in Japan. It cost £2,000,000 to build and the first world championship meeting to be held there was in 1963. It is now recognised as one of the best-organized racing circuits in the world. The Japanese must have felt deeply gratified at the performances of their machines in the Suzuka Grand Prix of 1965 for the first three riders in each of the 50 c.c., 125 c.c., 250 c.c., and 350 c.c. races, with the exception of Mike Hailwood's MV, rode Japanese machinery.

Japan's other major circuit is Fisco, also called Fuji, on account of its proximity to the volcano. The Japanese Grand Prix—now, to the regret of many fans, discontinued—was held at this picturesque track in 1966, 1967 and 1968.

Racing in Britain takes place principally at Brands Hatch, Oulton Park, Crystal Palace, Mallory Park, Scarborough, Castle Combe, Snetterton, Cadwell Park

163 The crowds strain forward as the riders race away from the start at Sachsenring—a 350 c.c. race in 1965.
164 Sachsenring.

165 One of the most popular short circuits in Britain, Brands Hatch in Kent, and the start of the 'Hutchinson 100', with Hailwood's 250 c.c. Honda already breaking away.
166 Brands Hatch.

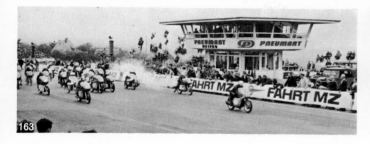

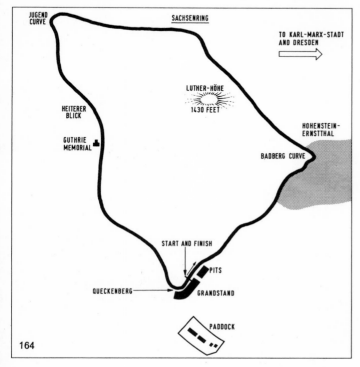

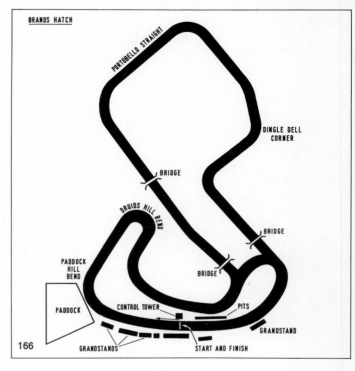

and Silverstone (which for many years housed the important Hutchinson 100 meeting). To Mallory goes the distinction of providing the biggest winner's purse in the British motor-cycle calendar, 1,000 guineas for a single event; though Brands Hatch is perhaps most generally regarded as the best and most exciting circuit in the country. This one-time grass-track racing centre is pleasantly situated and provides excellent facilities for spectators. Brands Hatch was to gain in stature with the passing of the years and this Kent circuit held the first motor-cycle event ever to be shown publicly on television in Britain—a grass-track meeting in 1947. By September 1949 work had already started on converting the grass track into a road circuit for cars and motor cycles. During the winter of 1951-2 the track was resurfaced with a non-skid material and John Surtees at the opening of the season raised the lap record to 69.6 m.p.h. It was during 1952 that an experimental race was held with the riders travelling in a clockwise direction, and so successful did this seem to be that, from then on, this was the regular way round at Brands.

John Surtees made a big name for himself racing at Brands, before going to the international meetings and then on to car racing, and, in 1953, Derek Minter, who was to succeed him as King of the Kent circuit, made his racing debut there.

In the winter of 1953-4 the track was extended—to 1.24 miles—from midway round the Paddock Hill bend, up Pilgrims Rise and round Druids Bend to rejoin the original circuit at the Bottom Straight. At the opening meeting John Surtees on a Norton recorded an average race speed of 67.76 m.p.h., witnessed by almost 45,000 fans.

Since those days Brands Hatch has been periodically improved and, following its acquisition by Grovewood Securities in 1961, the paddock club house, the restaurant and a number of shops have been added. Brands Hatch has a reputation which now extends among riders both inside and outside Britain, and is regarded by many of them as one of the premier race circuits of the world. And a further extension of the track now gives a 2.65 mile lap when required.

A DAY AT DAYTONA

The Daytona speed circuit in Florida and the year 1964 are immediately associated with the remarkable double success of Mike Hailwood when he broke the world one-hour record at 144 m.p.h. in the morning, and then went on to win the United States 500 c.c. Grand Prix, in the afternoon, raising the lap record and establishing a race record. Either success, taken separately, would have been a notable achievement. Together, they left no doubt that history was being made.

Seven years earlier Bob McIntyre's superb ride on a 350 c.c. Gilera at Monza had set the world hour record at 143 m.p.h.—a magnificent performance unmatched for its sheer brilliance. The worthiness of the new record was not so much the higher speed—after all, it was less than 2 m.p.h. faster than McIntyre's record—but the way in which it was attempted and accomplished.

The decision to make the attempt, taken by Mike's father during the previous night, was not known to Mike himself until he woke that February morning. The machine was hurriedly prepared before breakfast by Mike's Italian mechanic Vittorio Carruana and sprint specialist and motor-cycle sport reporter Charlie Rous. The tyres were changed, the fairing refitted and a high gear sprocket put on. Rider and machine had, in fact, terrifyingly little preparation. The MV on which the new record was established was hardly more than an impoverished practice machine, lacking the higher gearing and 'dustbin' fairing permissible under the international regulations governing the record attempt. These additions alone, Mike's father estimated, would have given him a 10 m.p.h. boost.

In the presence of FIM officials, Mike was off. That first lap—136.5—was a long way short of the 145 m.p.h. aim. At quarter time he was lapping 146.5 m.p.h. and had pulled the average up to 141 m.p.h. With 30 minutes gone, and 30 minutes to go, the average had moved to 142.9 m.p.h... still not good enough. Mike's father held up a sign which urged him on. With just 15 minutes to go the record had been overhauled with the average now at 145.2 m.p.h. but there was no room for jubilation for the average was now beginning

167 The 250s roar off at the start of Daytona's punishing
100-mile AMA championship race in March, 1967.
168 Daytona Speed Circuit, Florida.
169 Daytona Beach really *is* by the sea: the old beach course.

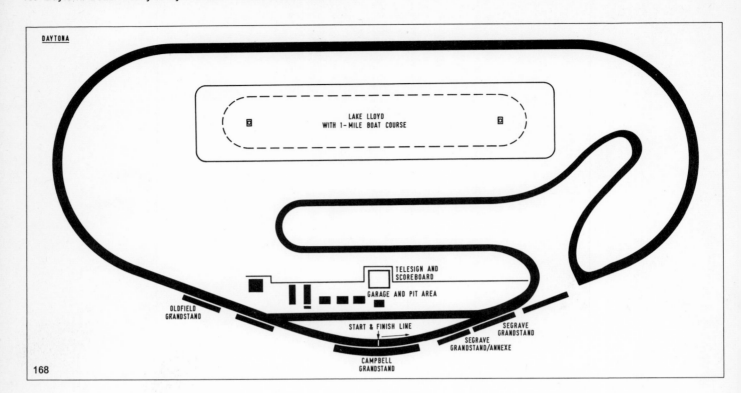

DAYTONA

LAKE LLOYD
WITH 1-MILE BOAT COURSE

TELESIGN AND
SCOREBOARD

GARAGE AND PIT AREA

OLDFIELD
GRANDSTAND

START & FINISH LINE

SEGRAVE
GRANDSTAND

SEGRAVE
GRANDSTAND/ANNEXE

CAMPBELL
GRANDSTAND

168

to slip back again, as Mike lost a second, maybe two, on each lap. But then it was all over and Hailwood dismounted, having raised the record to 144.8 m.p.h.

In the afternoon Mike was in the saddle once more, competing in the United States Grand Prix. Before him, a gruelling 127 miles round the Daytona circuit against some tough opposition—including a new sensation, the South American racer Benedicto Caldarella on a Gilera 4. Caldarella stayed close to Hailwood for 14 laps, but then Mike moved ahead. Eventually, gear-box trouble put the Gilera out of action and the Argentinian's challenge was spent. So far ahead had Hailwood and Caldarella thrust during those first 14 laps that Phil Read on a Matchless, who finished in second place, was lapped twice by the champion. The first American home was Bud Parriott, who rode sixth. Hailwood established a new race speed record of 100.16 m.p.h. and a new lap record of 103.3 m.p.h.

The famous Florida track on which Hailwood scored his double victory houses America's biggest road race each year, the Daytona 200-miler, organised by the American Motorcycle Association. The 750 c.c. side-valve Harleys used to dominate the race, but a strong Triumph challenge and a move from the 2-mile track to the 3.8-mile circuit brought British machines much more into the picture. Their success in 1967 gave each factory two victories over the big circuit. The Daytona speed bowl contrasts sharply with European circuits. An American rider once described its sweeping straights

as 'producing little more than freak drag races with riders tucked in under the paintwork, their engines bawling themselves silly in top cog'. But however Daytona is individually assessed, there is no doubting its prestige. In 1967 Yamaha, competing on an official basis for the first time, joined the Harley-Davidsons of America and the British Triumph and BSA entries to give the event an international flavour.

Against this background, American rider Gary Nixon netted £3,000 for his two major wins—the 200-mile race on the British works Triumph and the 100-mile race on a 250 c.c. Yamaha. Nixon won the 200-mile classic at a record speed of 98.23 m.p.h. exactly 2 m.p.h. better than the previous best, also set up on a Triumph the year before by Buddy Elmore, who rode second in the 1967 event. Only Nixon and Elmore completed the 53 laps. Triumph's success is even more commendable when it is remembered that the AMA rules allow 750 c.c. side-valve machines to complete against 500 c.c. bikes with overhead valves, though Fred Nix's 140 m.p.h. plus during a qualifying lap was unquestionably good going for a side-valve twin.

The Japanese impact during this qualifying lap was little short of astonishing. Conceding 150 c.c. to the British bikes and 400 c.c. to the Harley-Davidsons, Mike Duff's new 350 c.c. Yamaha racer finished eighth and reached a maximum speed of 132 m.p.h. to qualify. Overall final placings of the Yamahas ridden by Tony Murphy and Duff, were eighteenth and nineteenth.

170 A. G. Chapple on Daytona beach in 1909.

171 Another American speed-star: Joe Walter seen here with his Harley-Davidson twin at the Speedway Park in Maywood, Illinois.

172 Bart Markel, three times American National Champion, on his Harley-Davidson KR-TT.

169

170

171

172

173 Speed and sunlight: Isle of Man 1968.

174 The 500 c.c. Dutch Grand Prix, Assen, 1968.
Left to right: Waterfield (13), Auerbacher (4), Attenbergh (6),
Harris (12) and Enders (1), all on BMWs.

175 The AMA riders hurtle round the first left-hander of the
twisting 3.81 mile Daytona course in the 1968 200.

176 Dick Hammer's Triumph makes a quick pit-stop in the 1967
Daytona 200; he eventually finished 7th.

173

174

175

176

177 Before the start of the 1964 50 c.c. US Grand Prix: number 5 is Mitsuo Itoh, and beyond him are Isao Morishita (Suzuki) and Luigi Taveri (Kreidler).

178 2 February 1964: Charlie Rous, himself an ex-world record holder, checks the tyre pressures of Mike Hailwood's MV, just before Mike rides off to a new one-hour record of 144.8 m.p.h.; watching are FIM officials and, on the extreme right, Mike's father, Stan.

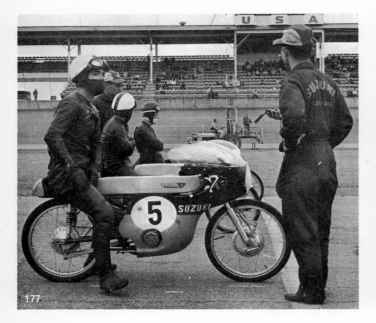

Mike Duff was excited by the 350 Yamaha's performance. He told *Motor Cycle* afterwards: 'The three-fifty was simply fantastic. It had so much power that it could easily stay with the five-hundreds, but I missed not having a fifth gear. For the big race, machines may not have more than four speeds. I had to make do with an ultra-high bottom gear which caused me to lose between two and four seconds a lap round the two tight corners'. Notwithstanding the effect of a strong headwind the 350 c.c. averaged 132.77 m.p.h. for just one lap of the speed bowl! Downwind, it was doing over 140 m.p.h. revving to 9,500 r.p.m.

International racing over the years has suffered from a lack of American-European contact, principally because of an internal situation in the United States where two representative bodies have existed. The American Motorcycle Association reflects the majority interest, and is not affiliated to the International Federation. In 1967 came the best hopes so far that the AMA would join the FIM, who control the world championships. With this hope realised, European riders would be able to compete freely in America in the Daytona '200', and the road would be clear for American aces to ride in Europe.

For two years the Harley-Davidson organisation had to play second fiddle to Triumph in the important Daytona 200-mile race. Then, in 1968, Cal Rayborn of San Diego, California, put the American machines back on top with a fine ride astride the latest version of the H-D 750 c.c. side-valve twin.

He not only thundered to victory: in doing so he crashed the magic 100 mile-per-hour barrier for the first time in the history of this remarkable American

179 Stan Hailwood gives Mike the thumbs-up sign as he whirls round Daytona in his one-hour record attempt.
180 Hailwood (second from right) is presented with the USMCC trophy for his victory in the US Grand Prix (1964).

181 The Daytona International Speedway in Florida, where all the great American aces race, including Gary Nixon, Cal Rayborn and Bart Markel. Daytona is the venue for the great American 200-mile race that bears its name.

event—his average speed being 101.29 m.p.h. There were 107 starters for this 53-lap race held on the 3.81-mile Daytona International Speedway circuit. Rayborn dominated the race. He moved to the front on the third lap, overhauling fellow Harley-Davidson rider Roger Reiman, and forged well ahead.

Once in his stride the handsome Californian was never very seriously challenged.

Rayborn had the fastest Harley in the race, capable of a top speed of 155 m.p.h. and he was certainly the outstanding road racer in the Harley-Davidson team. His race speed record was more than 3 m.p.h. faster than Gary Nixon's record the previous year on a Triumph. The Harley-Davidsons have enjoyed their share of success in American racing: Bart Markel for instance, was three times American champion between 1964 and 1967.

Although the following year Gary Nixon took the title on a Triumph, positions 2, 3 and 4 were all occupied by Harley-Davidson riders. Also in the top 10 that year was Cal Rayborn, but down at number 8. He had fewer than half the number of points which Nixon collected to take the championship; and of the individual events, Cal triumphed in only one—the 110-mile Indianapolis. But one of the great attractions of motor cycle racing is its unpredictability and in 1968, during the Daytona '200' at any rate, Cal Rayborn was the man of the moment, showing his style, skill and daring to thrilling effect. To get anywhere in American motor cycle racing you have to be a great all-rounder. The National Championship, sponsored by the American Motorcycle Association, is won by the professional rider who scores the most points in a series of events which includes

speedway half-mile and mile dirt-track events, road races and TT races—in America a dirt-track with artificial bumps. Bart Markel won this coveted title three years running. Bart was born in Flint, Michigan and developed an interest in scrambles when he was 22. Within a year he had turned professional and did so well that within a further year the Harley-Davidson dealer in Flint sent the suggestion through the H Q that Bart was someone they really ought to see. The result was that Markel exchanged his BSA for a sponsored ride on a Harley-Davidson flathead. At Daytona, in his first race, he crashed, destroying his machine though escaping injury himself. The company, to Bart's surprise, simply gave him a new machine and this one he took greater care of. He became one of Harley-Davidson's most prominent riders. Bart Markel has been something of a character in American motor cycle sport. He was once quoted as saying: 'Nice guys don't win; I ain't a nice guy'. He has also gone to great pains to assure people that for him, racing is a business and not a sport. 'I'm there for the money' he once said. 'That's all.' But when you can win races the way Bart Markel has done, who cares?

Manufacturers accept the Daytona 200 as without doubt the most important road race that the sport has to offer. A win at the Florida track in this spectacular event virtually guarantees giant follow-up sales in the United States, which is at the present time the most lucrative market in the world. It is not surprising, therefore, that in contrast to the FIM-sponsored World Championships, there is no shortage of factory interest in the big American race. In 1968 nine teams had either full factory backing or good works support.

182 J. Griffiths and A. Lampkin struggle to the top of a steep incline during a scramble.
183 Alf Hagon, the first man to break the ten-second barrier for the standing quarter-mile.
184 Mud and determination—two essential ingredients of scrambling.

182

183

184

...63 ...e British and Russian Speedway teams at the start of their
five-match Test series at Wimbledon in 1965.
Barry Briggs (left), Jurij Tchekranov (centre) and Igor Plechanov
race for the lead at the first bend, with
George Hunter close on their heels.

THE SPORT AT LARGE

Although its advocates would assert that it is the most important and glamorous stratum of the sport, road racing is by no means the sole contender for rider participation and public interest. When looking outside the sphere of road racing, trials-riding comes immediately to mind as one of the founder activities. This leads inevitably to scrambling, or moto cross, which has its origin in trials-riding, and grass-track riding, which in the early 1930s looked to have a great future.

Meantime, on the other side of the world, stripped-down road machines were raced on a loose-surface track as a special attraction at the New South Wales Agricultural Show of 1923. Thus Australia gave birth to dirt-track racing, which was to grow far beyond the Australian continent and which developed from the late 1930s into the sophisticated sport of Speedway, exciting thousands of ardent followers and creating colourful personalities. Record-breaking over various distances and for various periods of time has proved an irresistible attraction since the earliest days, and the outright World Speed Record is so prestigious an event that it has captured the interest of manufacturers, oil companies and riders alike. To this formidable list can be added the increasing popularity of sprinting (or drag-racing, as the Americans call it) to make the world of motor cycle sport sufficiently varied to satisfy every individual taste.

SCRAMBLING

Britain invented scrambling: the many thousands of scrambling enthusiasts abroad have a group of clubmen in Camberley, Surrey, to thank for initiating a sport which they now so much enjoy. These clubmen had a new idea. They wanted to organize a Southern Trial, based on the Yorkshire Scott Trial, but without the observed sections which the Scott, in common with all trials, included. The Auto-Cycle Union disapproved of the idea in that form. They pointed out that it couldn't be a trial if it didn't include observed sections. The enthusiasts were undaunted. They'd call it something else then. It wasn't exactly a race, as the entire point of the idea was to ride over the roughest, toughest ground available. Little realizing what he was saying, one member suggested that the outcome of such a race would be 'a rare old scramble.' That first race was a punishing test. Of the 80 starters, almost half retired: but a great new sport had been born. Scrambling developed into a specialized sport only after the 1939-45 war. Before then exceptional all-rounders such as Graham Goodman, Len Heat and Alfie West dominated scrambling. With the sport becoming established on the Continent (known there as moto cross), the Moto Cross des Nations was inaugurated in 1947 and immediately there began a close struggle for supremacy between Belgium and Britain. In the 1950s, through superb exponents like Brian Stonebridge and Les Archer, Britain held an unqualified lead. Belgium faded and Sweden took up the challenge. In 1955 they gained the title for the first time, and so began a hard and closely-fought battle between the Swedish and British riders extending over many years. Britain recaptured the title in 1956 and retained it in

1957. Sweden won the following year. Anglo-Swedish rivalry has characterized the Moto Cross des Nations during the 1960s, though Britain started a run of success in 1963 when she took the title through the Rickman brothers and Jeff Smith. The same team repeated the success the following year, but for 1965 Vic Eastwood came in for Derek Rickman and the title once more came to Britain. The British team again showed its superiority in 1967 in an exciting battle in Holland when the Belgian team, riders eager to establish a revival, was leading after the first race. A six-point deficit at the start of the second and final race was wiped out and the British team finished ten points ahead of Sween, who improved their position to take second place.

In a storming second race the Belgian attack was weakened through machine trouble, and at half way Eastwood was in the lead. Jeff Smith romped home in fifth position and Dave Bickers, who had been stopped at the start with a blocked air-vent in his petrol tank and had restarted in thirty-seventh place, rode with tremendous skill, strength and courage to take seventh place, a magnificent ride. Team racing is the yardstick of the Moto Cross des Nations. The present formula was established in 1963. Riders contest two races, points being awarded to all riders who finish. The nation with the three highest scorers in each race is the winner. It is not sufficient, therefore, for an individual alone to be successful. Joel Robert won both races in 1964, but his Belgian team did not collect the title.

The 1966 contest was held in France, a nostalgic occasion, for it was France more than any other country which put postwar moto cross on the map. A French

186

187 Auguste Mingels of Belgium, here seen taking a fast turn on a Matchless, was winner of the 1953 Dutch Motocross Grand Prix, held at Norg.

188 The first ever *Moto-Cross des Nations*; the Hague, 1947.

189 Chris Horsfield, on a CZ, keeping close tabs on his nearest rival.

190 Jeff Smith (25), fighting to keep tabs on Rolf Tibblin of Sweden at Hawkstone Park.

191 Grass track racing at Cobham.
192 A competitor at the Ponderosa Hare Scrambles, Hi Vista, California.
193 Don Rickman on a Bultaco during the British round of the 250 c.c. Motocross at Halstead, Suffolk, 1967.

194 The field of an English scramble waiting for the starter's signal.
195 Peter Gaunt wrestles with his 118 c.c. Suzuki
over the Foyers section of the 1967 Scottish Six Days' Trial.
196 Wayne Briggs (Exeter) hotly pursued by New Zealander
Bill Andrews (Poole).

194

195

196

197 Dave Bickers (6), Vic Eastwood (10) and Arthur Lampkin (7)
are among the leaders at the start of the first race in the 1966
500 c.c. *Moto-Cross des Nations* at Remeland in France.
They went on to gain a fine team victory for Britain.

197

businessman called Roland Poirier commercialized the sport by staging meetings on the outskirts of Paris in the immediate postwar period and made a major contribution to the booming, emergent sport which was to elevate moto cross into what it is now, the most international of all the motor cycle sports. Today British moto cross stars face a nine-month programme of events, with the Grandstand BBC TV Trophy rounds during the winter months. Although the sport had earlier been enthusiastically supported, it wasn't until 1952 that the FIM organized a European championship for machines up to 500 c.c. In the first round of that first year, Victor Leloup of Belgium on an FN machine was third. He rode with increasing success to become the first European moto cross Champion. It wasn't until the fourth round that Britain had her first triumph, when John Avery on a BSA, won the round held in Sweden. John Draper on a BSA brought the European Championship to Britain for the first time in 1955. Two years later a 250 c.c. European championship was established, and at the same time the 500 c.c. European was upgraded to world status. This was in recognition of the growing popularity of the smaller machines and in later years the 500 c.c. class was to be seriously threatened as a continuing class because of the under-capacity but light-weight machines—the 360 c.c. CZ for instance. (A solution to this problem has been put forward—the switching of the big machines into a 750 c.c. class.) From its almost insignificant beginnings, moto cross has developed into a mass spectator sport and in Britain, particularly, its extensive television coverage and the winter Grandstand events have created a widening interest among the general public. There is a compulsive attraction about seeing men on motor bikes skidding and sliding through mud and slush. Success demands physical strength and an astonishing capacity to keep a machine moving against the challenge of seemingly impossible odds. As Dave Bickers puts it: 'Nowadays, to get anywhere in the results, and especially in the grands prix, you must go flat out over every part of the course. I found early on in my racing career that beyond a certain speed a bumpy section of track will give a smoother, safer ride if you hit it really fast.'

Bickers is undoubtedly one of Britain's best-ever scramblers. He joined the Greeves team at a time when they were developing really good scrambling machines and in 1960 he won his first European title, repeating the success the following year. Jeff Smith, many critics agree, is the greatest scrambler Britain has produced. His intelligent and calculated approach to the sport

198 Joel Robert of Belgium in full flight on a 250 CZ.
199 Many critics consider Jeff Smith
to be the greatest scrambler that Britain has ever produced.

200 Arthur Lampkin (BSA) John Banks (BSA) and Paul Friedrichs
(CZ) bunched together ahead of the rest of the field
during the second race of the 500 c.c. British
Moto-Cross Grand Prix at Farleigh Castle in July 1967.

201 Vlastimil Valek of Czechoslovakia.
202 Victor Arbekov of the USSR, the
first Russian 250 c.c. Moto-Cross champion.
203 Denis Westwood (5) Bill Turner (3) and Len Crane (1)
with their respective partners.

204 O.L. de Lessa cornering hard in the MCC Gymkhana
at Brooklands, June 1910.
205 Trials rider Stevens with a relaxed and comfortable-looking
passenger, tackling Butter Tubs Pass, August, 1913.

comes as a revelation to those who think moto cross calls for nothing more than bull strength and a bonehead capacity for charging across the roughest ground at the greatest possible speed. He says: 'The only time it is important to lead the field is when crossing the line at the end of the last lap. I am content to stay in about seventh or eighth place until the leaders have sorted themselves out.' It's a philosophy that brought Jeff Smith a world championship for the first time in 1964, riding his BSA machine. Jeff's natural ability over the rough has developed from his skill in trials-riding, which was his first love, but the technique of scrambling has to be learned well. Says Jeff: 'The feeling of control which you acquire through trials is essential for high-speed scrambling.'

There's an international flavour about moto cross and each country has developed its own personalities —Joel Robert of Belgium, Rolf Tibblin of Sweden, Paul Friedrichs of East Germany, Victor Arbekov of the Soviet Union, Vlastimil Valek of Czechoslovakia, Arne Wickstrom of Finland, Mogens Pedersen of Denmark, Jan Heyboer of Holland and Alfred Benzak of Austria, while in Britain names like Smith, Bickers, Vic Eastwood, Chris Horsfield, Arthur and Alan Lampkin and the Rickman brothers, Derek and Don, have captured a substantial family following through the Saturday afternoon Grandstand events. The scramble that started it all, way back in 1924, was won by Arthur Sparkes and one of the men competing on that occasion was Les Archer. Les' son was to turn to scrambling after making a name for himself in road racing, and, with a few stars of the 1950s, help to establish moto cross at a European level, and so fashion Great Britain's major rôle in the sport's development.

201

202

203

TRIALS

Many successful racers have learnt the basis of their craft through trials-riding. Trials are by no means the most glamorous or affluent sector of the sport, but to enjoy any kind of success requires controlled riding technique, unity with your machine and a sensitive feeling for balance. You've also got to ride intelligently, thinking out the trial carefully if you want to avoid shedding points unnecessarily. The reward is personal satisfaction in doing a difficult job and doing it well. The peak prestige event in the calendar is the International Six Days Trial, usually held in a different country every year. Riders from a variety of countries take part. It's a gruelling test for both machine and rider. Over all kinds of terrain, competitors will cover some 200 miles daily, split into various sections. Time schedules between check points form the basis of marking and marks quickly mount against the rider for excess time.

206

Britain founded the International in 1913. This was the age before the specialist rider and this first International, which attracted some 170 competitors, was won by a three-man British team which included the irrepressible Charlie Collier, winner of the first TT, but this time driving a Matchless sidecar outfit. Trials captured the active interest of riders from many countries. For instance, when the ISDT was held in Britain for the first time in seven years (1961), twenty nations were represented among the 270 starters. The most consistently successful competitors in the ISDT in recent times have been the East German contingent on their sensational MZ machines. In 1967 the event took place in Poland and the East Germans secured top honours for the fifth consecutive year.

Most trials, though, last only a few hours and are over short courses comprised of the most difficult terrain available in the area—mud, sand, rocks, hillocks. Unlike the ISDT, there are no time schedules to bother with. Speed is not important; losing valuable marks in the observed sections is. They can be lost for putting one or both feet on the ground, and five marks are forfeited for failing to keep your machine going. Machine adaptation is simple: lightweight, manoeuvrability, correct gearing and plenty of power at low engine revolutions are the requirements.

In Britain the one name synonymous with trials riding is Sammy Miller, who was once a keen road racer, successful in many events in his native Ireland and in more important races. He is now, indisputably, the top star in 'mud plugging', and on his 500 c.c. Ariel and 250 c.c. Bultaco machines has won almost every important trial in the calendar. Gordon Jackson, a Kent farmer, was another big name in trials riding. With just one penalty mark—the lowest ever recorded up to that time—he rode his 350 c.c. AJS to victory in the 1961 Scottish Six Days Event. Among other 'greats' in postwar years—names that will always be recorded in the history-books—are Hugh Viney and Bill Nicholson.

209 The Bemrose Trial, March, 1966. Ron Langston and Doug Cooper on the 497 Ariel were runners-up.

210 Bemrose 1967; Sammy Miller clears Hawks Nest beneath watchful and critical eyes.

211 The Suzuki 250 c.c. twin prototype tested at the Scottish Six Days Trial for later use in the 1967 ISDT.

212 The 1966 Greeves Anglian with standard forks.

213 A Bultaco, resting between events at Tweseldown.

210

211

212

213

GRASS TRACK

214 A trotting course in the United States, converted to the needs of an early grass-track event; picture taken in 1913.
215 High Beech, Epping Forest, 1928: Speedway makes its British debut before an audience of 30,000.

Grass track racing, though faithfully supported by enthusiastic riders and followers, is also devoid of the big-time glamour atmosphere given to road racing. Yet few will deny the particular excitement and thrill engendered by this branch of motor cycle sport.

In terms of mass recognition, grass tracking suffers from the absence of powerful financial backing from which can develop well-publicized competition at a European and International level. This branch of the sport is very much alive in Britain, however, and there has been an encouraging revival of interest recently. Grass tracking dates back to the 1920s. A decade later Brands Hatch, Kent, now the popular short-circuit road race venue, contributed to its development with regular meetings. Jack Surtees, father of motor cycle and car champion John, was a favourite at Brands, in those days, along with another immortal name in motor cycle sport, Eric Oliver.

In the 1930s another favourite track was at Layham's Farm, also in Kent, where the circuit was on a hillside. Hence Layham's became known as a mountain grass track. In recent years, Alf Hagon was the dominant force, taking the 350 and 500 c.c. national titles in 1954. He duplicated this amazing double success in 1962. More recently the names of Malcolm Simmons, Dave Baybutt, Tony Black and Don Godden have made a major impact on the sport. Godden won his first national title in 1965 at Braintree and he has been successful against virtually every top European rider. He has won well over 500 events in Britain and abroad. Black has also done well in European contests. His international debut was in 1963 and by 1966 he was winning a succession of races on the Continent.

As in speedway, the JAP power unit remains supreme for grass track machines. This engine dates back to the 1930s and remains basically the same today.

214

216

215

217

218

216 Grass-track racing, Brands Hatch, 1939. Riders waiting for the start in the paddock.
217 The line-up for the start of a 350 c.c. scratch race at Brands Hatch, 1933.

218 Brands Hatch again. The start of a 250 c.c. scratch race.
219 Dave Baybutt (No. 26), Pinhard Prize Winner, laps R. Nash.
220 Dave Hunter and Ivan Kitching, on a Triumph outfit, winning the 1965 national title from Mick Webster and John Justice.
221 Alf Hagon corners inside Reg Luckhurst.

219

220

221

SPEEDWAY

222 Tiger Stevenson returns to West Ham for the 1930-31 season.
223 Lionel van Praag, the first man to achieve the distinction
of World's Speedway Champion, Wembley, September 1936.
On the right, Eric Langton, who finished second,

Speedway projects an atmosphere and excitement which is unique. The close-combat conditions of a short circuit, the churlish rasp of engines, the deliberate broadsiding and the wide, up-swept handlebars—not to mention the keen team competition—have given speedway a fan-following akin to football. Spectators attend regularly to encourage their home teams and in doing so form a liaison with the track and its riders unequalled in any other branch of the sport.

It is probable that Speedway has its origins in America as early as 1910-11 when racing motor cyclists took over the horse-trotting tracks for their new sport. Then came the closed-circuit race at the New South Wales Agricultural Show—now generally recognised as the identifiable beginnings of speedway. Enthusiasm was quickly aroused and dirt-track racing spread rapidly across Australia. It was introduced to Britain by a meeting at the High Beech in Epping Forest in 1928. No sport could have wished for a more successful debut.

The event was expected to draw about 3,000 spectators. Over ten times that number were attracted. They were not disappointed: the Australian ace Billy Galloway gave the public a spectacular demonstration, and the broadside technique, which was to be an integral part of dirt-track riding, thrilled and astonished them. Within months regular meetings were being held in various parts of the country, and it was not long before about fifty tracks were operating.

This was speedway's barnstorming era of flying cinders and trailing broadsides. At first, and into the early 1930s, riders from Australia and America drew the crowds, but later British and European stars were appreciated for their skill and daring.

Such was the international nature of dirt-track racing that the first world championship was held under the auspices of the FIM in 1936. Riders from Australia, Sweden, New Zealand, Germany, Canada, France, America, Denmark, Spain and South Africa competed, and

222

and on the left, Bluey Wilkinson who, although winning all his heats in the final, beating both Langton and Praag, only finished third, owing to the bonus system in the qualifying rounds.
224 The brothers Cordy and Jack Milne photographed in April 1936.

225 The start of the first heat in the World Speedway Championships at Wembley, 1965. Left to right, Ove Fundin (Sweden), who finished third, Leif Larsson (Sweden), Nigel Boocock (Great Britain) and Lubos Tomicek (Czechoslovakia).

after tying on the number of points, Australian Lionel Van Praag won the run-off against Eric Langton of Britain to secure this first world title. Jack Milne from the United States won the 1937 championship and it was Australia again in 1938, this time through Bluey Wilkinson. The war inflicted a temporary retirement, but the enthusiasm for dirt-track racing lay only just below the surface and at the end of hostilities there was an immediate upsurge of interest. The revival was remarkable. British soldiers, awaiting demobilization as members of the occupying army, thronged the Hannomag track in Germany, and similar circuits which were quickly established. The world championship was continued in 1949 and Tommy Price brought England her first international honours that same year. Wembley Stadium was to become the recognized venue for the world championship final, though Sweden was host country in 1961, 1964 and 1966. During the last decade the overall dominance of such riders as Ove Fundin of Sweden and Barry Briggs of New Zealand has left little room for other countries to secure much of a hold on the championship. Russia has challenged in recent years and Igor Plechanov was second in 1964 and 1965. England's last champion was Peter Craven in 1962. Peter is recognized as one of the great riders of all time. He was killed in September, 1963, while racing in Edinburgh.

In such a specialized sport, machines have to be specialized, and the JAP overhead valve engine has found almost absolute acceptance. It is basically simple, is easy to work on and produces the required power at comparatively low engine revs. There have been a number of attempts to follow the example of the JAP engine, but by far the most successful has been the ESO from Czechoslovakia's CZ concern. This has been used with success by Russian and Polish teams, and of course by Barry Briggs.

For the speedway spectator, however, machines have

223

224

225

226 29 July, 1947. Jack Parker leads Lionel van Praag (Australia) and Norman Parker (England).
227 Split Waterman leads Ove Fundin at New Cross Stadium.

always taken second place to the rider—to a degree that is perhaps somewhat unusual in a sport which has such a high reputation for the technical knowledge and understanding of those who support it. In speedway the thrill and the excitement of the race is all-important and this means that attention, almost to the exclusion of all else, is focused on the rider. This has encouraged a showmanship quality about some of the most popular riders. The first 'personality' was Split Waterman, who exploded on the speedway scene in 1947 after sand racing in the Middle East. Although there was some of the charm of the old-time pirate in the gay Waterman character, his skill as a speedway rider was never obscured. He won many honours, but never succeeded in claiming a world title. He was nearest in 1951 when Australia's Jack Young beat him.

Whenever speedway is discussed, one man's name is certain to be included: Barry Briggs. No-one has enjoyed such recognition. No-one inspires such enthusiasm among his fans. Briggs won his first world championship in 1957, repeated his success in 1958. The following year he was placed third, second in 1962, and then back with top honours in 1964 and 1965.

Barry, New Zealand-born, started riding in 1951 and moved to Britain in 1952 with an urgent desire to go places in the speedway business. His early rides were crude and clumsy and he fell many times. First he rode for Wimbledon, then New Cross: he joined the Swindon team in 1963. From then on he began to move fast. He is the only speedway star to make a strong impact on the world outside the track and his wide-spread fame brought him success in national popularity polls— a tribute to the outstanding place he has commanded within the sport over many years.

One of Briggs' keenest rivals has been the sensational Swedish rider, Ove Fundin. He alone has won more

world championships than Barry. He established this distinction in 1967 by gaining the title for the fifth time, though Briggs might even the score in 1968, so close is the competition. Speedway on that occasion, as many times before, demonstrated its unpredictability. Russia's Igor Plechanov was tipped to take top honours and a cash prize of £1,000, but he finished the evening in fourth place while Barry Briggs, after falling in his first ride, could do no better than fifth. It was an evening which underlined the popularity of speedway: over 75,000 fans witnessed that final at Wembley.

SPRINTING

Sprinting is a highly specialized form of motor cycle sport. It is by no means new, but the impetus of the more commercialized drag-racing scene in the United States, plus the exciting deeds of British sprinters such as George Brown and Alf Hagon, have helped to capture an increasing following for the sport in recent times.

This form of racing is basically an acceleration test over a measured distance, generally a quarter mile. At a standing start, revs are built up and culminate in a tremendous and exciting blast-off. The rider lets in the clutch with a bang, the rear wheel spins and, as the bike streaks off, the tyre leaves a line of smouldering rubber on the track. The sprinter's art is in keeping the power full-on while holding the bike in a straight line.

Sprinting also takes in other distances and has 'flying' counterparts, like the kilometre and quarter mile. In Britain sprinting is done on disused airstrips and a few seaside promenades, but unimpeded stretches of concrete are not long enough to give competitors sufficient run-in and run-out to beat the best international timings for the flying mile. At Bonneville, with a run-in of three miles, the Salt Flats present the sprinter with conditions infinitely more suitable for the making and breaking of records.

The National Sprint Association was formed in Britain in 1958 and now arranges sprint meetings with competitions for all classes from 125 c.c. up to 1,300 c.c.—primarily racing machines, but there are also events for production and even vintage models. Its president, until his tragic death, was Donald Campbell.

Though basically similar, sprinting and drag-racing have essential differences. Sprinting is a race against the clock, even if other competitors are taking part at the same time. Drag-racing is more a contest, often between a couple of racers. In drag-racing, the fastest rider could be the loser—he might, for instance, make a bad start and therefore be second-best across the finishing line.

The deeds of American dragsters like Clem Johnson, with his big Vincent, the Negro Sonny Scott, whose machine is powered by two 650 c.c. Triumph engines, and Boris Murray, with an exciting 1,300 c.c. Triumph which he raced at 191.3 m.p.h. to make it the world's fastest unstreamlined motor cycle, are known among

231

sprint and drag-racing fans the world over.

On the British side of the Atlantic, George Brown, president of the National Sprint Association, Alf Hagon, Martin Roberts and Fred Cooper are the king pins. A few years ago, Brown reckoned that the time for the standing quarter mile could be reduced to nine seconds or less and that his beloved Super Nero machine might well get down near to that timing on a really good strip. George had been told by Americans Don Garlets and Tommy Ivo that on drag strips in the United States, where rubber is built into the asphalt for extra grip, his machine would have no trouble in regularly clocking runs in the nine-second region.

But it was Alf Hagon who bettered Brown's 10.42 seconds record in July 1967 to become the first Briton to crack the 10-second barrier. Alf's supercharged 1,260 c.c. vee-twin JAP engine spluttered and floundered about the 440-yard line while flying at nearly 150 m.p.h., but all was well. It was an eventful day for Alf. In his first run he almost lost control when he collected a flat tyre, but he kept the throttle wide open and recorded 10.15 seconds. Later in the day he streaked down

in 9.93 seconds to set the record (one way) for the Duxford strip.

Three weeks later at Duxford, his best was 9.86 seconds. Then, on 20 August at the British Hot Rod Association's meeting at Santa Pod, Bedfordshire, he pared the time down to 9.68 seconds. And, by an incredible coincidence, he again found himself fighting a flat front tyre!

For official recognition, all sprint records must be made in two directions, in two consecutive runs completed within an hour. At Elvington, Yorks, during a record-shattering weekend in October 1967, Hagon secured both the absolute world and national records under these conditions for the standing-start quarter mile with an average time of 9.95 seconds, at an overall speed of 90.4 m.p.h.

Perhaps the sprinter with the biggest incentive is Fred Cooper. If he can reach a speed of 200 m.p.h. in Britain with his supercharged 1,300 c.c. Triumph-powered Cyclotron, the London *Daily Express* has agreed to sponsor an attempt by Fred on the all-out world speed record at the Bonneville Salt Flats.

THE BMW MIRACLE

Wilhelm Noll's success in becoming the world 500 c.c. sidecar champion in 1954 was the start of what was to become the most firmly-entrenched class domination in contemporary road racing. Every year since, without interruption, the world sidecar champion has driven a BMW-powered outfit. The parade of star riders is legendary—Noll, Faust, Hillebrand, Schneider, Fath, Deubel, Scheidegger and Enders, and they are all German or Swiss.

The Bavarian factory was weaned on motor cycle sport and developed an insatiable appetite for racing. In the 1920s the BMW horizontally-opposed twin-cylinder engine was almost inconsequential when first mounted in solo racing machines, but development work painstakingly continued and was rewarded just before the second World War when, supercharged and with telescopic front forks and rear springing, these BMWs tamed the declining Nortons and Velocettes. Finally, in 1939, Georg Meier scored his unique TT victory. The ban on superchargers after the war crippled their efforts in the solo classes and they were unable to recapture their pre-war eminence, in spite of attracting the attentions of star riders like Geoff Duke and Walter Zeller.

In the outright speed record-breaking business, the BMW is associated with a period of glorious history through the indefatigable Ernst Henne whose 174 m.p.h. on a supercharged BMW in 1937 was not beaten

234 O. Ley with the then new 500 c.c. ohc single-cylinder
BMW in 1936.
235 Ernst Henne with his 500 c.c. works machine, 1926.

236 Henne in the supercharged BMW-Rekordei, being
pushed out for his record-breaking run along the
Frankfurt-Darmstadt autobahn in October 1937; his final
speed was 174 m.p.h., and the record stood for fourteen years.

234

235

236

237

during the next fourteen years! Until 1954 Nortons and Eric Oliver were a dominant force, leaving little room for others in the sidecar championships. Their combined strength gave Britain victory from the start of the championships in 1949 until 1953, except for Cyril Smith's success in 1952, which was also established with a Norton.

Then Noll came along. From then on it was BMW all the way. Walter Schneider was West Germany's first double champion in successive years in the sidecar event, a remarkable and historic achievement though Oliver had made the hat-trick earlier. His successes were in 1958 and 1959. A strong man physically, and a dominant personality, Schneider's driving, with passenger Hans Strauss was always impressive. It was forceful and determined and he liked to move to the front at the start of the race and stay there. After his 1958 triumph, Schneider said he would retire but he came back in 1959 to win the championship for the second time. This 'retirement announcement' seems endemic

in the road racing breed but there have been so many reappearances after such pronouncements that retirements, when concerning a man of less mature years, are accepted with scepticism. Schneider threatened retirement on a number of occasions, again at the end of his successful 1959 season, but this time he was adamant and has not been seen in the world classics since.

Indomitable BMW, from the standpoint of preserving their invincibility, were not unduly disturbed by Schneider's disappearance, for by this time Helmut Fath was making a most favourable impression. In 1960 he fitted his own fuel-injection system to the engine and again the title went to West Germany. Helmut, some drivers would tell you, was typical of the Continental approach to racing and lacked a certain finesse which many purists prefer to see. His thrusting technique and very fast engines, however, paid off. In 1961 he sustained injuries at the Nürburgring and again in the Isle of Man TT. As a result the championship was secured by Max Deubel—on a BMW.

237 Eric Oliver and his Norton with passenger Bliss during TT practice in 1955; this was the year that BMW first unseated the powerful Oliver/Norton combination from its dominance of the sidecar championships.

238 Georg Meier flies his supercharged horizontally-opposed twin-cylinder BMW to victory in the 1939 Senior TT. This was BMW's last important win with solo machines.

239 BMW sidecar team Hillebrand and Grunwald crash spectacularly on the Hockenheim circuit in 1956.

238

239

240 The Enders/Engelhardt combination in their BMW during the Dutch TT sidecar event. Assen 1967.

241 The supercharged twin on which Georg Meier won the 1939 Senior TT. This machine was brought to England from France, having been stolen from Germany during the occupation, and completely restored by M.L.G. Motorcycles, the British BMW distributors.

242 Max Deubel in his 492 BMW keeps very adjacent to the kerb. Brands Hatch, 1966.

240

243 Walter Schneider and Hans Strauss of West Germany,
sidecar champions for BMW in 1958 and 1959.
244 Geoff Duke with a BMW in 1958.

245 Fritz Hillebrand and Manfred Grunwald rounding
Signpost Corner on the Isle of Man circuit in 1957,
the year they won both the TT and the world championship.

Max was born in Cologne in 1935 and took a passionate interest in 'chairs' in 1954. Four years later he won a national Junior championship. His first significant performance, internationally, was in the 1959 Hockenheim Grand Prix when he took third place, and he was the 1961 TT winner at a record speed. He repeated his 1961 world championship success in 1962, 1963, and 1964—a unique performance in the sidecar class so far. The contribution to this outstanding record made by passenger Emil Horner was fully acknowledged in Deubel's own modest way. Indisputably sidecar-racing is a team effort, and the uncanny feeling for a race which both Deubel and Horner shared, and their mutual understanding and harmony, was a major contribution to their phenomenal run of success.

The smooth, streamlined sidecar outfits of today are gleaming sophisticates when contrasted with the comparatively unscientific 'open-fronted' chargers of yesteryear. The BMW engine gives considerable power compared with others of similar capacity and this, combined with its low overall height, makes an ideal unit for the modern layout.

Some of the sport's most spectacular thrills have been provided by the sidecar men, and one incident to make its mark in the history of racing occurred in the 1967 TT when West Germany's Siegfried Schauzu suffered the indignity of having his passenger, Horst Schneider, fall out! But the German's BMW outfit not only raced on to win the TT, but in doing so established a record speed of 90.96 m.p.h. It happened on the final lap at Governor's Bridge. Schauzu braked especially hard—he'd been racing against keen competition from Klaus Enders and Rolf Englehardt—and Schneider slid out, but rapidly dived back on to the platform with nothing more than a cut chin to prove it had all happened.

The BMWs completely dominated the race. Georg Auerbacher, with Ernst Dein, retired, but only after racing the fastest lap at 91.7 m.p.h. BMW outfits occupied the first five places—with German crews in 1st and 2nd positions and British crews in 3rd, 4th and 5th.

How different forty-four years earlier when the first sidecar TT took place. Then only fourteen outfits were entered—against the eighty-four entries of 1967! Douglas had three machines there, Norton, Scott and Sunbeam two each. Freddie Dixon, riding a Douglas 'banking outfit' which was described at the time as an 'ingenious device which enabled the whole machine to be leaned over to the right or left as required' was the winner, with Graham Walker and George Tucker, both on Nortons, second and third. The outright superiority of BMW in world sidecar events now spans well over a decade, and is still unchallenged.

246 BMW team Noll and Cron; they were using this only partly enclosed fairing style as late as 1954.
247 World beating combination Fritz Scheidegger (Switzerland) and John Robinson (England).

248 Max Deubel and Emil Horner, four times world sidecar champions, in the rain at Brands.
249 Helmut Fath shoots across Governor's Bridge in the 1967 TT.

WORLD RECORD ATTEMPTS

Since the late nineteenth century when Gottlieb Daimler raised eyebrows with his historic two-wheel boneshaker, there has been special honour and glory reserved for he who could claim to be the fastest man on two wheels. Recorded claims to be the world's fastest go back to 1909. Speeds mounted from 75 m.p.h. steadily upwards until April 1920, when an American, Ed Walker, riding a 994 c.c. Indian twin at Daytona Beach, USA, is credited with 103.5 m.p.h.—the first to beat 100 m.p.h.

But there is a slight doubt whether this and earlier speeds were officially authenticated. By 1921, though, the battle was on, and riders such as Bert Le Vack, Claude Temple, Freddie Dixon, Oliver Baldwin and Joe Wright became famous for their success in hoisting the officially-recognised speed for the flying kilometre and flying mile higher and higher. By 1930, Wright, riding an OEC Temple, had exceeded 150 m.p.h. Up and up went the speed with the German, Ernst Henne, breaking the record more often than anyone else.

Then in the United States once more, and on what was to be a sensational day in August, 1956, Wilhelm Herz climbed inside his enclosed NSU twin-cylinder supercharger to add more than 25 m.p.h. to the earlier record. His official timing: 210 m.p.h. This was his best performance during that August visit to the Bon-

250 Bob Leppan standing beside his super-streamlined Gyronaut X-1 (1966).

251 Joe Wright of London on his £5,000 AJS just before attempting to break the world motor cycle speed record at Southport Sands, Lancashire, in 1933.
252 Noel Pope being given instructions by a cameraman.

neville Salt Flats, Utah; two days earlier he had, in fact, taken the record to 189 m.p.h. with a 350 c.c. machine.

There were vast differences, speed apart, from the record secured by Walker in 1920 and Herz' triumph thirty-six years later. The most striking perhaps were between the machines on which the two records were established: with the machine and rider enclosed the NSU had a supercharged 499 c.c. power unit developing 110 b.h.p., while the early Indian was a traditional bike of 994 c.c. with no streamlining. While Walker's record was almost a solo endeavour, Herz achieved his success with an entire organization and an entourage of back-room boys, the recognized accompaniment of German attempts.

Though Herz held the official world record, he was not the fastest two wheel racer. American Johnny Allen, with a cigar-shaped machine looking more like a projectile than a motor cycle, had done a couple of runs at 193.72 m.p.h. under the American Motorcycling Association's timings—unfortunately not recognized by the FIM—and while Herz left the Bonneville Salt Flats to go home, Allen stayed on to prepare for yet another attempt. This time his sophisticated Thunderbird engine, running on alcohol fuel and encased in its sleek glass-fibre shell, recorded 214.17 m.p.h., but the record was not officially recognized. From then on, it was the United States all the way, first in September 1962 through Bill Johnson with a 649 c.c. Triumph engine in a remarkable machine which looked more like one of Malcolm Campbell's early racing cars than a two-wheel record breaker. Then came Bob Leppan with his extreme example of design technology combined with a power unit consisting of two 650 c.c. Triumph engines. During the American Motorcycle Association's speed week at the Bonneville Salt Flats in 1966, Bob piloted this super-streamlined Gyronaut X-1 at 245.67 m.p.h. to raise the unofficial record by more than 21 m.p.h. His fastest of the two runs was at 247.76 m.p.h.

Leppan was a 28-year-old Triumph distributor in Detroit at the time of his record bid and came to the world record through plenty of drag-racing experience. His success was an ambition which had taken twelve years to fulful, and was shared by Jim Bruflodt as chief designer and engineer of the Gyronaut, and Alex Tremulus, who designed the glass-fibre, cigar-shaped body. When racing this phenomenal machine, Leppan is more of an astronaut than a traditional motor cyclist. He lies well back in the cockpit and his space-helmeted head rests against a padded cushion. Bob Leppan has been fascinated by the history of speed all his life and as a boy read with great excitement of

the records established by racers such as Henry Segrave and Malcolm Campbell. As a motor cycle dealer it was not surprising that he found an outlet for his passionate interest in speed in two-wheel record attempts. Years before he had been in pedal-cycle racing; then he became fascinated by the mechanical side of cycling, particularly after owning his first motor cycle, a Triumph T20 Tiger Cub. Original plans for the Gyronaut included the use of a gyroscope for stability, but this feature was later dropped, though the name was retained, with suitable adaptation. The two engines were mounted in tandem style and produced 140 b.h.p. on methanol, or 200 on nitro-methane fuel. It had a four-speed standard gear box and the standard clutch, with additional plates, was sufficient for the combined engines pulling a top gear of approximately 2:1.

The underlying misfortune about the speeds established by Bob Leppan is that they, like those of Johnny Allen previously, were under the auspices of the American Motorcycling Association and are therefore not recognized by the FIM, the authority for motor cycling throughout Europe and most other parts of the world outside America. So officially, according to the FIM, and in spite of Leppan's remarkable success, the world speed record remained at the 224.5 m.p.h. recorded by Bill Johnson in his 649 c.c. Triumph at Bonneville in September 1962. The highly sophisticated machines necessary for these outright world-speed records are extreme and highly advanced and in all except name bear little resemblance to anything suggested to the average enthusiast by the term 'motor cycle'. Not so the record-breaking machines of old. These chargers were identifiable as motor cycles and were ridden by all-rounders whose names were very often known for racing round tracks as well as for record-breaking attempts. Record-breaking in the less contrived days of the early 1920s, for instance, was more fun than business. At the famous Brooklands track there were special 'record' days towards the end of the racing season, and it was on one of these days, in 1923, that Claude Temple on his 996 c.c. British Anzani increased the 'world's fastest' to 108 m.p.h.

There was nothing very special about his machine, although it had been built specially for record breaking attempts. It was a 'wee twin', with a single overhead-camshaft to each cylinder, with a bore and stroke of 78 × 104 m.m. The bumpy Brooklands circuit was not ideal ground for such an attempt, and the combination of machine and circuit gave Claude's record a significance well merited, though it created little interest.

Greater interest there might well have been had a prophet foretold the significance of the occasion, for as it happened, this was to be the last world record set up at the famous Brooklands track. Temple, though, was to recapture the record at 121.5 m.p.h., but at the Arpajon course in France, in 1926, after Bert Le Vack, a well known Brooklands racer, had recorded 119 m.p.h. on his 998 c.c. Brough Superior JAP in 1924.

The Arpajon course was a stretch of good racing road south of Paris and the French authorities had no objection to closing their highways for these record-breaking attempts. The surface was excellent and Bert was not unduly troubled in improving on Claude Temple's Brooklands record.

There were still eight years before Ernst Henne was to begin his four-year reign as speed king of the world, and during that time the mantle switched from Temple to Oliver Baldwin, to Le Vack, then on to Ernst Henne. During a three-month period in 1930 British rider Joe Wright and Henne were to lower the record on three occasions—Wright first at 137.32 m.p.h. on an OEC; Henne a few weeks later at 137.66 m.p.h.; and Wright again at 150.74 m.p.h. set up this time in Ireland. Then came the sensational display of record-breaking by the combined might of BMW machinery and Ernst Henne talent. Britain's dominance, cracking over the previous two years, was finally shattered. The Henne epoch began at the Tat course in Hungary in November 1932, but first tribute must be paid to Joe Wright's sensational 150.5 m.p.h. world record established on a 998 c.c. OEC Temple JAP fitted with a streamlined front fork and, for the first time, a supercharger. His superb performance beat Henne's best by at least 13 m.p.h. and was to remain intact for almost two years. Claude Temple worked with Wright on these record-breaking attempts and he shrewdly observed that conditions were infinitely better for such attempts if competitors could avoid the 'circus' atmosphere which they inevitably engendered. There were usually a number of riders waiting their turn and this 'crowd' situation, with the time pressures it imposed, was not always conducive to the best performance. He privately hired a stretch of road just outside Cork and announced Wright's two-day bid on the record.

The Englishmen suffered acute misfortune. Rain during the first day made riding impossible and although conditions improved on the second and final day, the gremlins had not completely departed. At the start of Wright's first run an engine shaft sheared and valuable time was lost while a second engine was fitted.

Then Wright was off on his first run and easily bettered Henne's 137.5 m.p.h. He prepared for the second and final run, more optimistic now, but his bad luck persisted: a timing official got in the way and accidentally broke the timing tape. Joe, undaunted, started all over again and made two more stupendous runs—one at 152.48 m.p.h. and the other at 149 m.p.h. to establish the record at 150.74 m.p.h.

Britain thus relinquished the world title in a blaze of glory and—except for Fernihough's 169.5 m.p.h. established in Hungary in the spring of 1937 and held for just six months—departed the world speed scene for good. A successful bid in November 1932 started Ernst Henne's record-breaking reign. From that time until 19 November 1937 and except for a twelve-month period when Fernihough, and then Piero Taruffi of Italy, bettered the German's record, he proudly carried the title of the 'fastest man on two wheels'. On four occasions he improved on his own performance, raising speeds by 21.5 m.p.h. to 173.5 m.p.h. All the records were established on the outstanding BMW. First he went to Hungary in 1932 and added 1.5. m.p.h. to Wright's record. Two years he eased it up to 153 m.p.h. In 1935 he found a new stretch of road near Frankfurt, Germany, and on the 735 c.c. BMW added a further 6 m.p.h. to push the record to 159 m.p.h.

Britain was reluctant to yield her place in the record-breaking world and Claude Temple, his interest well sustained though he himself had long since retired as a rider, had only a few months earlier taken his Zenith JAP machine and rider Claude Atkins to Belgium in the hope of taking the world speed title back to Britain: but that expedition failed. Meantime, Henne's record was exposed to increasing potential competition and he realized something special was needed if he was to raise the record significantly.

He returned to the Frankfurt road in 1936 and with a fully-streamlined BMW of only 495 c.c. shattered his own record by 10 m.p.h. Despite its wind-cheating shell, the machine was not heavy and had only one brake, which acted on the transmission shaft. Henne also sported a streamlined helmet, the rear portion of which tapered almost to the middle of his back!

The final successful British challenge came from Eric Fernihough on a 998 c.c. Brough Superior JAP. Eric had seen Ernst's streamlined BMW and as a result did not favour the fully-encased shell, which got Henne, said Fernihough, into some appalling wobbles at times. Admittedly he increased the streamlining on his own machine, but avoided the full-enclosure, maintaining it was essential to keep the front wheel in the air stream. He departed for Hungary, hired a stretch of good road and after having his record attempt witnessed only by Hungarian guards and a few officials, returned home well pleased: he'd improved on Henne's 169 m.p.h. by just 0.77 m.p.h.

254

255

256

256 The revolutionary Triumph 'cigar' machine
in which Johnny Allen (right) broke the world record
with 214.4 m.p.h. on 6 September, 1956. Standing with him are the
designer 'Stormy' Maugham (left) and tuner Jack Wilson.

257 Bill Johnson in his 649 c.c. Triumph at Bonneville,
where he established the 224.569 m.p.h. record on 5 September, 1962.
His machine was an unsupercharged parallel twin,
developing nearly 80 b.h.p., and that streamlined
body is 17 feet long.

A freak machine from Italy challenged Fernihough's record six months later, though it was given little chance save by those closest to it. It was a 492 c.c. Gilera, a four-cylinder supercharged Rondine-engined machine of almost incongruous design. It was an unusually tall structure and the rider sat almost upright. It was fully encased and, completing its bizarre appearance, a huge fin dominated the rear. Popular Italian rider Piero Taruffi was chosen as pilot and on a stretch of road between Brescia and Bergamo he actually captured the title for Italy with a speed of 170.5 m.p.h. But within a few weeks the title was back with the racing phenomenon, Ernst Henne. With comparative ease he added 3 m.p.h. to establish the last record before the outbreak of war. Reluctant still to accept Britain's diminishing rôle in the sphere of ultimate world speed record-breaking, Eric Fernihough went to Hungary again in 1938 in a final attempt to recapture prestige for Britain. The bid ended tragically, for Eric was killed. The war ended Ernst Henne's historic contribution to world speed record-breaking. The early days of rugged, open machines which broke records with a brashness easily reconcilable with the pioneer period of motor cycle history, had long since gone. Streamlining had been introduced and had developed into complete encasements for both machine and rider.

Postwar world speed attempts were not only of a different era, but were soon dramatically seen to be. Within a few years of Wilhelm Herz's first postwar record established in Germany at 180 m.p.h., the Bonneville Salt Flats were to become the obvious venue for the big-deal record attempts and the motor cycle was destined to lose its identity completely under nose-to-tail streamlining. Herz held that first postwar record for four years, but then New Zealand took the title for the first time through Russell Wright, whose expert handling of his 998 c.c. Vincent pushed the record to 185 m.p.h. In so doing he won a £1,000 prize offered by *Motor Cycle*, the London-based magazine, for the first Briton on a British machine to capture the record.

The American Salt Flats were now to become the happy hunting ground for the record seekers and Wilhelm Herz's 1956 visit with his NSUs coincided with the unveiling of Johnny Allen's astounding 'cigar' machine—a revolutionary design so spectacular that the motor cycle world was staggered. Meantime, Johnny tucked himself quietly away into the cockpit and flashed across the flats at a never-before-seen 214 m.p.h. The new era had arrived. It was a spectacular occasion. Allen sat between the handlebars and engine, the handlebars having been extended to make it possible for him to steer. Although the projectile stretched to 15 ft. 8 in., its width was only 22½ in. and it was fortunate that Allen was slim enough to climb inside. The man behind the project was former pilot 'Stormy' Mangham, who developed the entire concept from the basis of a three-year-old British Triumph Thunderbird 650 c.c. production machine. And the future? In 1966 Bob Leppan was reported to be working with his team on a four-engined machine aimed at more than 300 m.p.h., and in 1967 he went to Bonneville again determined to raise his 245.67 m.p.h. American mile record to at least 250 m.p.h. with his Gyronaut X-1, but conditions were unsatisfactory. The salt was wet and the temperature of 100 degrees cut power drastically, though the machine did 245.33 m.p.h. on a first practice run.

In under fifty years the world speed record on two wheels has moved from just over 100 m.p.h. to (unofficially) 245 m.p.h.—an increase of nearly 150 m.p.h. Although that 300 m.p.h. target of Bob Leppan's appears somewhat speculative, is the 55 m.p.h. more which he needs to achieve his ambition so outrageous?

257

OFFICIAL WORLD SPEED RECORDS

Date	Rider	Country and course where record set		Machine	m.p.h.
14.4.20	E. Walker	U.S.A.	Daytona	994 c.c. Indian	103.5
9.9.23	F.W. Dixon	France	Arpajon	989 c.c. Harley-Davidson	106.5
6.11.23	C.F. Temple	England	Brooklands	996 c.c. British-Anzani	108.5
27.4.24	H. Le Vack	France	Arpajon	998 c.c. Brough Superior JAP	113.5
6.7.24	H. Le Vack	France	Arpajon	998 c.c. Brough Superior JAP	119
5.9.26	C.F. Temple	France	Arpajon	996 c.c. OEC Temple	121.5
25.8.28	O.M. Baldwin	France	Arpajon	998 c.c. Zenith JAP	124.5
25.8.29	H. Le Vack	France	Arpajon	998 c.c. Brough Superior JAP	129
19.9.29	E. Henne	Germany	Munich	740 c.c. BMW	134.5
31.8.30	J.S. Wright	France	Arpajon	998 c.c. OEC Temple JAP	137.5
21.9.30	E. Henne	Germany	Munich	740 c.c. BMW	137.5
6.11.30	J.S. Wright	Ireland	Cork	998 c.c. OEC Temple JAP	150.5
3.11.32	E. Henne	Hungary	Tat	735 c.c. BMW	152
28.10.34	E. Henne	Hungary	Gyon	735 c.c. BMW	153
27.9.35	E. Henne	Germany	Frankfurt a / M	735 c.c. BMW	159
12.10.36	E. Henne	Germany	Frankfurt a / M	495 c.c. BMW	169
19.4.37	E. Fernihough	Hungary	Gyon	998 c.c. Brough Superior JAP	169.5
21.10.37	P. Taruffi	Italy	Brescia-Bergamo	492 c.c. Gilera	170.5
28.11.37	E. Henne	Germany	Darmstadt	493 c.c. BMW	173.5
12.4.51	W. Herz	Germany	Munich	499 c.c. NSU	180
2.7.55	R. Wright	N. Zealand	Christchurch	998 c.c. Vincent HRD	185
2.8.56	W. Herz	U.S.A.	Bonneville	347 c.c. NSU	189
4.8.56	W. Herz	U.S.A.	Bonneville	499 c.c. NSU	210
5.9.62	W. Johnson	U.S.A.	Bonneville	649 c.c. Triumph	224.5

ROAD RACING WORLD CHAMPIONS

Solo Classes 50 c.c.

1962	Ernst Degner, West Germany (Suzuki)
1963	Hugh Anderson, New Zealand (Suzuki)
1964	Hugh Anderson, New Zealand (Suzuki)
1965	Ralph Bryans, Ireland (Honda)
1966	Hans-Georg Anscheidt, Germany (Suzuki)
1967	Hans-Georg Anscheidt, Germany (Suzuki)

125 c.c.

1949	Nello Pagani, Italy (Mondial)
1950	Bruno Ruffo, Italy (Mondial)
1951	Carlo Ubbiali, Italy (Mondial)
1952	Cecil Sandford, Britain (MV)
1953	Werner Haas, W. Germany (NSU)
1954	Rupert Hollaus, Austria (NSU)
1955	Carlo Ubbiali, Italy (MV)
1956	Carlo Ubbiali, Italy (MV)
1957	Tarquinio Provini, Italy (Mondial)
1958	Carlo Ubbiali, Italy (MV)
1959	Carlo Ubbiali, Italy (MV)
1960	Carlo Ubbiali, Italy (MV)
1961	Tom Phillis, Australia (Honda)
1962	Luigi Taveri, Switzerland (Honda)
1963	Hugh Anderson, New Zealand (Suzuki)
1964	Luigi Taveri, Switzerland (Honda)
1965	Hugh Anderson, New Zealand (Suzuki)
1966	Luigi Taveri, Switzerland (Honda)
1967	Bill Ivy, Britain (Yamaha)

250 c.c.

1949	Bruno Ruffo, Italy (Guzzi)
1950	Dario Ambrosini, Italy (Benelli)
1951	Bruno Ruffo, Italy (Guzzi)
1952	Enrico Lorenzetti, Italy (Guzzi)
1953	Werner Haas, W. Germany (NSU)
1954	Werner Haas, W. Germany (NSU)
1955	Hermann Müller, W. Germany (NSU)
1956	Carlo Ubbiali, Italy (MV)
1957	Cecil Sandford, Britain (Mondial)
1958	Tarquinio Provini, Italy (MV)
1959	Carlo Ubbiali, Italy (MV)
1960	Carlo Ubbiali, Italy (MV)
1961	Mike Hailwood, Britain (Honda)
1962	Jim Redman, Rhodesia (Honda)
1963	Jim Redman, Rhodesia (Honda)
1964	Phil Read, Britain (Yamaha)
1965	Phil Read, Britain (Yamaha)
1966	Mike Hailwood, Britain (Honda)
1967	Mike Hailwood, Britain (Honda)

350 c.c.

1949	Freddie Frith, Britain (Velocette)
1950	Bob Foster, Britain (Velocette)
1951	Geoff Duke, Britain (Norton)
1952	Geoff Duke, Britain (Norton)
1953	Fergus Anderson, Britain (Guzzi)
1954	Fergus Anderson, Britain (Guzzi)
1955	Bill Lomas, Britain (Guzzi)
1956	Bill Lomas, Britain (Guzzi)
1957	Keith Campbell, Australia (Guzzi)
1958	John Surtees, Britain (MV)
1959	John Surtees, Britain (MV)
1960	John Surtees, Britain (MV)
1961	Gary Hocking, Rhodesia (MV)
1962	Jim Redman, Rhodesia (Honda)
1963	Jim Redman, Rhodesia (Honda)
1964	Jim Redman, Rhodesia (Honda)
1965	Jim Redman, Rhodesia (Honda)
1966	Mike Hailwood, Britain (Honda)
1967	Mike Hailwood, Britain (Honda)

500 c.c.

1949	Les Graham, Britain (AJS)
1950	Umberto Masetti, Italy (Gilera)
1951	Geoff Duke, Britain (Norton)
1952	Umberto Masetti, Italy (Gilera)
1953	Geoff Duke, Britain (Gilera)
1954	Geoff Duke, Britain (Gilera)
1955	Geoff Duke, Britain (Gilera)
1956	John Surtees, Britain (MV)
1957	Libero Liberati, Italy (Gilera)
1958	John Surtees, Britain (MV)
1959	John Surtees, Britain (MV)
1960	John Surtees, Britain (MV)
1961	Gary Hocking, Rhodesia (MV)
1962	Mike Hailwood, Britain (MV)
1963	Mike Hailwood, Britain (MV)
1964	Mike Hailwood, Britain (MV)
1965	Mike Hailwood, Britain (MV)
1966	Giacomo Agostini, Italy (MV)
1967	Giacomo Agostini, Italy (MV)

Sidecar Class 500 c.c.

1949	Eric Oliver, Britain (Norton)
1950	Eric Oliver, Britain (Norton)
1951	Eric Oliver, Britain (Norton)
1952	Cyril Smith, Britain (Norton)
1953	Eric Oliver, Britain (Norton)
1954	Wilhelm Noll, W. Germany (BMW)
1955	Wilhelm Faust, W. Germany (BMW)
1956	Wilhelm Noll, W. Germany (BMW)
1957	Fritz Hillebrand, W. Germany (BMW)
1958	Walter Schneider, W. Germany (BMW)
1959	Walter Schneider, W. Germany (BMW)
1960	Helmut Fath, W. Germany (BMW)
1961	Max Deubel, W. Germany (BMW)
1962	Max Deubel, W. Germany (BMW)
1963	Max Deubel, W. Germany (BMW)
1964	Max Deubel, W. Germany (BMW)
1965	Fritz Scheidegger, Switzerland (BMW)
1966	Fritz Scheidegger, Switzerland (BMW)
1967	Klaus Enders, W. Germany (BMW)

ACKNOWLEDGMENTS

AJS Motorcycles
Johnny Allen
M. Carling
Castrol Limited
Central Press Photos Ltd.
Cycle World, Calif. U.S.A.
Daytona International Speedway Corporation
Fédération Française de Motorcyclisme
Fox Photos Ltd.
Wolfgang Gruber
Brian A. Holder
Keystone Press Agency Ltd.
George Lynn
London Express News and Feature Services
T. C. March
Trevor Meeks
Michelin Tyre Co. Ltd.
M. L. G. Motorcycles
Montagu Motor Museum
Moto Guzzi
Motor Cycle; London
Motor Cycle News
Motor Cyclist Magazine, Calif. U.S.A.
Hans Harmsze, Motor Foto-Dienst
B. R. Nicholls
NSU
Popperfoto
Radio Times Hulton Picture Library
Volker Rauch
Rex Features
Karl Schleuter
Science Museum, London
Shell International Petroleum Co. Ltd.
Sport & General Press Agency Ltd.
Vic Stacey
Syndication International
Erwin Tragatsch
Triumph Motorcycles
The Vintage Motor Cycle Club
Larry Willett
David Burgess Wise
Kurt Wörner
Haydon Young
Andrzej Zielinski

INDEX

Page numbers in italics refer to illustrations.